This book is dedicated
to all the fine people who ever
worked for *Southern Living*,
and to all the readers who ever
picked up a copy.

Southern Living

50 YEARS

A CELEBRATION OF PEOPLE, PLACES, AND CULTURE

Introduction by Sid Evans
By the Editors of *Southern Living* with Valerie Fraser Luesse

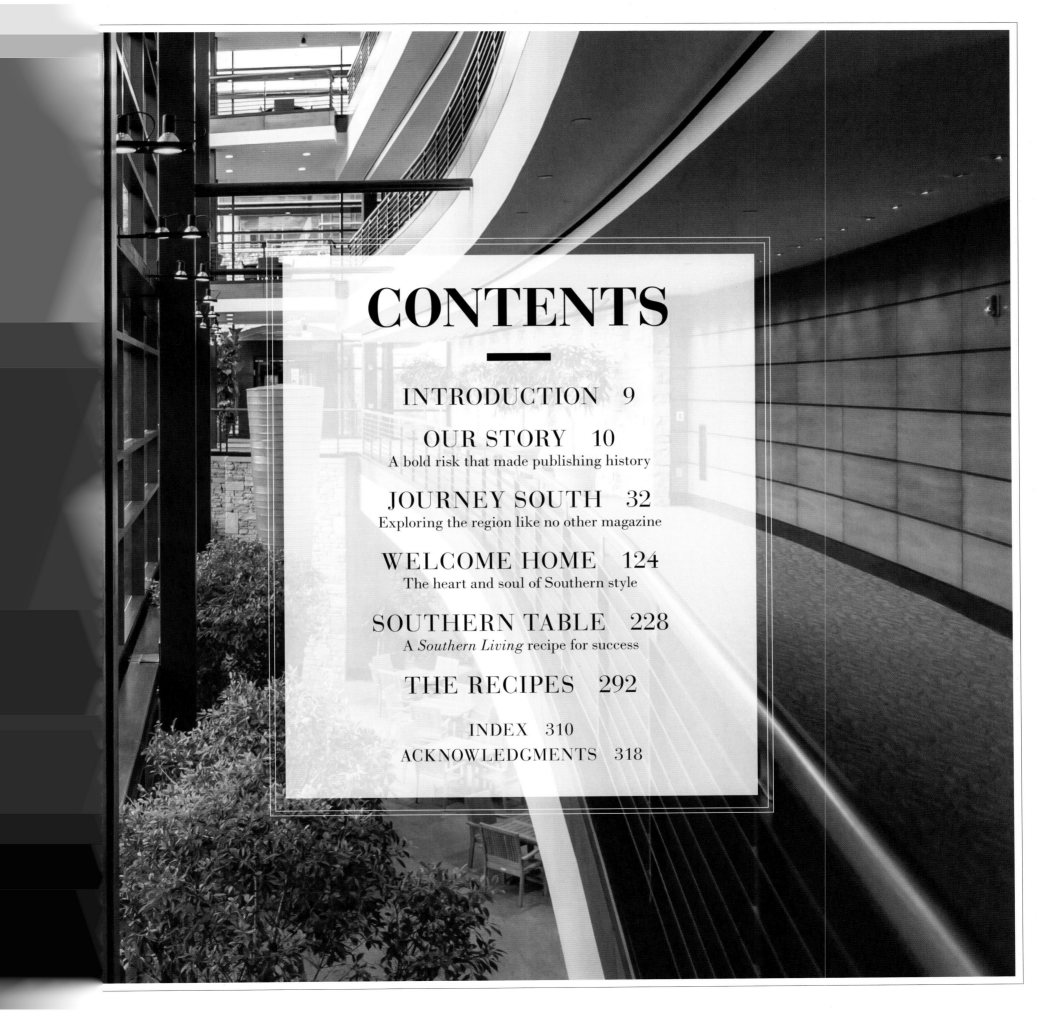

CONTENTS

—

FEBRUARY 1966—25¢

Southern Living

AN EDITION OF THE PROGRESSIVE FARMER

HOUSTON--Giant of the South

NEW FURNITURE
From Southern Manufacturers

1,000-Mile AZALEA TRAIL

Fertilizers for Southern Lawns

CHICKEN-*Party Style*

The first cover of *Southern Living* was photographed at the home of J.F. Pate in Mobile, Alabama. Jo Anne Magnes Fusco and her friend Alice McMurphy Jones were riding a bicycle for two when scouts for the magazine spotted them and asked their parents for permission to take their picture.

A CELEBRATION

THIS BOOK is not just a celebration of the 50th Anniversary of *Southern Living*, a milestone the magazine will hit in February 2016. It's a celebration of the South, a heartfelt tribute to our people, places, and culture. It represents the work of a lot of talented people over a lot of years, but it's not a history book, and it's by no means a definitive guide to the region. This is a scrapbook, a collection of covers, photographs, and stories that attempt to capture the beauty and sweep of the South as seen through the eyes of its biggest fan.

It's also the story of an incredible journey that started in February 1966, when The Progressive Farmer Company launched *Southern Living*, declaring it the "Magazine of the Modern South." This was a bold statement for an upstart publication, especially one born into the racial conflict and violence of the 1960s, but *Southern Living* was relentlessly focused on the positive when no one else was. The magazine championed the region's food, homes, gardens, cities, arts, literature, and natural beauty, turning the lens away from politics and current events to address everyday Southern life. The editors envisioned a bright future for the South, and they promoted that vision on every page.

It wasn't always smooth sailing, but *Southern Living* survived more than one identity crisis (and some questionable covers) because it stayed true to a very simple idea: The magazine had to stay Southern. "It must and will be in every issue as thoroughly Southern as crepe myrtle, longleaf pine, Mardi Gras, fig preserves, and black-eyed peas," said an early prospectus. Within five years, *Southern Living* was in the black and growing fast. Within 10 years, it had quietly become one of the biggest and most profitable magazines in the country. In 1985, its parent company, Southern Progress Corporation, sold to Time Inc. for just under $500 million, then the most ever paid for a magazine business.

We haven't strayed far from the vision laid out by our founders in 1966, but what has changed is the South. I imagine those *Progressive Farmer* editors would be surprised and delighted to know that our cities are the most diverse, dynamic, and sought-after cultural destinations in the country, that there is a nationwide obsession with Southern cuisine, or that handmade Southern products have paved the way for a whole new economy in artisanal goods. They would be especially pleased that the South is celebrating its agrarian roots, with a new generation of farmers reminding us all where we came from.

—Sid Evans, Editor in Chief,
Southern Living

Covering the South

Southern Living Travel would have to produce miles and miles of copy as the magazine took off and began localizing its editorial with multiple editions. Pictured with Editor Gary McCalla (far left) and Managing Editor John Logue (center) are (from left) Travel Editor Caleb Pirtle, Travel Assistant Karen Lingo, and photographer Gerald Crawford in 1970.

OUR STORY

"We are not all things to all people.
But to our readers, we are
all things Southern and good."

Any new magazine is a gamble.

Will readers embrace it? Will advertisers pay for it? There's only one way to find out, and it's expensive. ◆ Given 50 years in print and almost 16 million readers, *Southern Living* turned out to be a shrewd risk that paid off more than anyone could have imagined. But when it first appeared in February 1966, the odds were stacked against it. ◆ The magazine was aimed squarely at Southern cities and suburbs, yet it would be launched by The Progressive Farmer Company, whose editors had spent their careers covering cotton, cattle, and soybeans for Southern

Visionaries

In 1908, *The Progressive Farmer* and *Southern Farm Gazette* merged, laying the foundation for a successful agricultural publishing company. Joining forces were (from left) Dr. B.W. Kilgore, John S. Pearson, Dr. Clarence Poe, Dr. Tait Butler, and Eugene Butler.

Farm Teams
(Above) The 1892 staff of The Progressive Farmer Company. Seated on the left is J.W. Denmark, son-in-law of *The Progressive Farmer* founder, Col. Leonidas L. Polk. Editor J.L. Ramsey is reviewing the paper. The four men standing in back are printers, while the man on the far right is an assistant, called a "printer's devil."

(Right) In 1911, a thriving The Progressive Farmer Company moved from Raleigh, North Carolina, to Birmingham, which was a major rail hub more centrally located within the region.

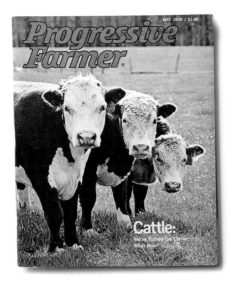
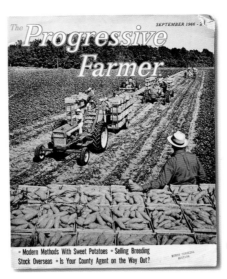
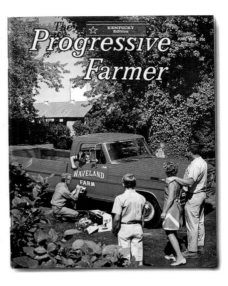

Ahead of Its Time
The Progressive Farmer Company pioneered localized editorial and advertising, publishing multiple editions targeted to farmers in different agricultural regions.

farmers while offering recipes, dress patterns, and homemaking advice to rural women in *The Progressive Farmer* magazine. Privately held, with just a few families owning the lion's share of stock, the company was firmly rooted in the South and intended to produce *Southern Living* not in New York or any other major publishing center but in Birmingham, Alabama. And instead of recruiting a staff from national titles on the East and West coasts, it promised readers a magazine "by Southerners, for Southerners, and about Southerners."

Created to celebrate the best of the South, *Southern Living* premiered at the height of the Civil Rights Movement, when the entire region was in turmoil. Eugene Butler, who was president and Editor in Chief of the company when the magazine was launched, would later write that it was sometimes difficult even to persuade prospective staff to come to Birmingham and interview. Nobody watching the violence and racial conflict on the evening news back then would have been eager to relocate to Alabama—especially for a brand new magazine that might not survive.

Despite the obstacles, however, the publishers knew they had just two options: diversify or die. By the mid-fifties, the boom times for farm magazines had passed, and profit margins were shrinking. "What is the future of a magazine such as ours?" Butler would ask his Board of Directors in 1961.

The Progressive Farmer could trace its diminishing returns to a profound cultural shift that was happening in the South. Attitudes and lifestyles were changing as an agrarian economy gave way to an industrial one. Technology was making it possible to produce bigger crops with fewer people, so farms were shrinking in number but growing in size. As farming became more commercial, advertisers began pressuring *The Progressive Farmer* to abandon its home and family content and focus on the business of agriculture.

Workers who lost their jobs in the fields either moved to town or moved away to find work. With burgeoning metro areas like Dallas, Atlanta, Houston, and Washington, D.C., on the horizon, a region once blanketed with small towns and family farms was struggling to reinvent itself and take hold of its future.

The Progressive Farmer also faced an unusual circulation dilemma: It needed to relocate some of its readers. For decades, the old adage was that even in the hardest times, you could walk into any home in the rural South and find two publications: the Bible and *The Progressive Farmer*. Families subscribed for generations. Unfortunately, as more and more Southerners stopped earning their living from the land, *The Progressive Farmer* found itself with many subscribers who were not actively farming. That didn't sit well with advertisers, who were in the business of selling tractors, tools, chemicals, etc. The magazine needed to lure its nonfarm subscribers away from *The Progressive Farmer* without losing them altogether. But where to put them?

By the end of 1962, the publishers were quite convinced that the answer lay in a family magazine that could speak to the growing cities and suburbs of the South. That year, for the first time, two magic words appeared in the minutes of a company Board meeting: *Southern Living.*

Tapped to chair the magazine's development committee was Advertising Director Emory Cunningham. He was a rising star who would eventually lead and significantly expand the company. From the beginning, Cunningham had *Southern Living* in his blood. In August 1965, he sent Butler a memo that succinctly captured the spirit of the new magazine:

> *As I see* Southern Living, *it should be completely* <u>*Southern.*</u>
> *Not most of the time, not when advisable, largely or predominantly, but* <u>*completely*</u> *and* <u>*exclusively*</u> *Southern from cover to cover.*

The *Progressive Farmer* ad salesmen (and they were all men in those days) were elated by the possibility of *Southern Living* because it opened the door to lucrative consumer advertising and a definite boost, not just in company revenue, but in their personal earning potential. This well-established *Progressive Farmer* sales force was critical to *Southern Living.* It would have cost a tremendous amount of money to hire and train new salesmen and to assemble all the necessary market data on the South, which *The Progressive Farmer* already had. "Most assuredly, if we had

started *Southern Living* from scratch, it would have cost three or four times what it actually cost to establish the publication," Butler later wrote. "And we didn't have that kind of money."

Not all of their struggles were financial. There were editorial ones as well. Early on, the publishers were hoping *Southern Living* could do something no magazine had ever done—serve the entire family, appealing equally to men and women, with even an occasional nod to teenagers in the household. It would cover everything from fashion to sportfishing, home projects to hairdos.

"*Southern Living* magazine wanted to speak to Southerners in their own voice but didn't quite know what it wanted to say," explained John Logue, who joined the magazine in 1967 as Features Editor and went on to become Creative Director of the company. Early concept statements suggest the founders were more certain of what *Southern Living* was *not* than what it realistically could become:

> Southern Living . . . *is not a shelter book, a men's magazine, a women's service book, a general or travel magazine.*
> *It is an individual. . . .*
> Southern Living *is a family service magazine with no axe to grind, but always with a point of view. It will neither editorialize nor preach . . .*

That last point would become a bone of contention within "the family." By the time *Southern Living* was launched in 1966, *The Progressive Farmer* had been advocating for farm families for 80 years. The editors had published many "*Progressive Farmer* crusades," impassioned treatises on such causes as rural health care and education, national farm legislation, soil and water conservation—even air-conditioning. The magazine was unapologetically political, not in the sense that it endorsed any party, but in its willingness to take a vocal position on issues that affected its audience.

Recognizing how difficult it would be for farm editors who were steeped in those traditions to adapt to *Southern Living*, the publishers began looking outside for new talent to bring into the fold. Still, their own rural roots were so deep that some of them initially thought *Southern Living* would "promote better understanding between urban and rural people," as Butler wrote in the Editor's letter of the premier issue. And while he highlighted the food, homes, gardens, and travel that would become the pillars of *Southern Living*,

Butler expected the magazine to take on the "dirty air, filthy water, growing crime, traffic jams, noise, and tension" that could make life in cities "a frustrating and sometimes dangerous experience." For good measure, he quoted from the Psalms: "Behold, how good and pleasant it is when brothers dwell in unity!"

Having successfully crusaded for farmers, The Progressive Farmer Company expected an equally outspoken crusader in the suburbs, which *Southern Living*, in the end, refused to be.

Ad Man

Raised in rural Alabama, Emory Cunningham was a former Navy pilot who became a successful ad salesman at *The Progressive Farmer* and would eventually lead the entire company. Once the idea for *Southern Living* took hold of him, he became its unstoppable champion.

The young, liberal-thinking editors who came to Birmingham from places like Atlanta and Oklahoma City would advocate for a better South, but they would do it in their own way—simply by showing readers positive examples, which was a far cry from the crusades.

For inspiration, this new editorial team was looking west to *Sunset* magazine, determined to create something equally fresh and modern for the South. To pull it off, however, they needed to tap the cash reserves of their parent company. That meant Butler and a handful of major stockholders would have to gamble their family fortunes on this upstart of a magazine, which sometimes got entirely too big for its britches:

During its first year Southern Living
has been an expensive child.
Typical of the young, she has struggled to be
different from her supporting and protective
parent. Let us hope Southern Living *will be*
different. Also, let us hope she will develop
character worthy of her parent,
The Progressive Farmer.
—*"History of* Southern Living*,"*
Eugene Butler Papers, Southern Progress Corp.

Top Staff
Charles Walton shot countless successful food covers that fueled high newsstand sales.

It might be tempting to dismiss The Progressive Farmer establishment as overly cautious and hopelessly set in its ways. But the company had survived two world wars and the Great Depression, among other things, and had come through it all with enough money to launch *Southern Living* without borrowing a dime. They believed they knew what it took to survive in turbulent times: Look very carefully before you leap, and keep a vice grip on the purse strings.

They had at first hoped that *Southern Living* would be a reasonably manageable expansion of the existing Homes department in *The Progressive*

Style and Substance
Philip Morris came to *Southern Living* from Oklahoma in 1969. His passion for great architecture, historic preservation, and livable neighborhoods shaped the magazine's design philosophy.

Farmer, which they had renamed "Southern Living" in October 1963. The two could perhaps share content, covers, and even staff. A letter written many years earlier from then *The Progressive Farmer* Editor Clarence Poe to Mrs. W.H. Hutt, who became Homes Editor in 1913, seems prophetic in light of the bond *Southern Living* later forged with readers:

We want the women to feel that they are partners in the department, responsible for its success . . . and that the woman who edits it is not away above them but one of them. In short, we want them to feel that it is one great sisterhood . . .

The Homes department gave *Southern Living* a solid launchpad, but, ultimately, the magazine would have to chart its own course in order to succeed, and the tension between where it came from and where it needed to go was evident in the first issue. Beneath the *Southern Living* cover logo was the tagline "An Edition of *The Progressive Farmer.*" Inside the magazine, however, just above the table of contents, was a very different message: "The Magazine of the Modern South."

Identity crisis aside, *Southern Living* debuted to rave reviews from Southerners. They loved the magazine. More specifically, they loved the idea of a magazine that loved *them*:

This is exactly the type of magazine sorely needed. . . . I am weary of tongue-in-cheek slurs and that talked-down-to manner in anything written about Texas and Texans . . .
—G.B. Southernwood, Missouri-Kansas-Texas Railroad Company

If the quality of future issues matches the quality achieved in its first issue, Southern Living *doubtless will prove to be of great value to Southerners. It also may serve as a good-will ambassador to those outside the region who still think of the South as a benighted land*

of crackers, rednecks, and unreconstructed rebels dragged kicking and screaming into the twentieth century.
—Editorial Page, *The Richmond News Leader*

The July 1966 issue was the last one to carry *The Progressive Farmer* tagline on the cover. That same year, the Homes department in *The Progressive Farmer* was renamed "Southern Farm Living" and stopped sharing a cover with the new magazine.

Struggling to find its footing, *Southern Living* made its share of costly missteps. An ill-fated July 1967 issue reduced the page size during a slim advertising month. Readers let the magazine know that they felt cheated. *Southern Living* was losing money—$1 million and counting. And while there were multiple causes for its struggles, chief among them was the house divided that *Southern Living* still was, even a year into publication.

"Give Gary McCalla credit," said John Floyd, who succeeded McCalla as Editor in Chief. "His greatest contribution was that he was able to break away from the past and let *Southern Living* be what it needed to be."

Once McCalla became Editor in 1969, he anchored the magazine to the four pillars of food, homes, travel, and gardens and never allowed it to drift. He became famous on the staff for holding every story and photograph to the same litmus test: "What's Southern about it?" He was also relentless in demanding nothing but the best for his readers. Editors and photographers would sweat through story conferences, dreading McCalla's four-word death sentence for an an image: "What else you got?"

Southern Living really began to hit its stride in the mid-seventies and was off like a rocket by the end of the decade. The editors had learned to balance the aspirational and the practical while enthusiastically celebrating all things Southern— the perfect mix for their audience. Gradually moving away from "something for everybody"

journalism, *Southern Living* found its focus and its voice. Over time, it would position itself not as a family magazine but as a service-based lifestyle magazine speaking primarily to women.

Southern Living also made itself a valuable friend to Southern authors and columnists, inviting the likes of Pat Conroy, Fannie Flagg, Shirley Ann Grau, Ellen Gilchrist, Reynolds Price, Jerry Flemmons, Barry Hannah, Celestine Sibley, Rick Bragg, and many more into the magazine.

Perhaps most important of all, the editors figured out how to build a sense of community among readers by publishing their recipes, featuring their homes and gardens, and sending travel editors to explore their states firsthand. As McCalla wrote, upon the magazine's 20th anniversary, "We are family, *Southern Living* and the South."

The same family of readers who were loyal supporters of the magazine gave rise to a successful book company, Oxmoor House, which was incorporated in 1970. Four years later, the young publisher ventured into art books with

The Salesmen
Advertising leader Jim DeVira (holding Champagne) led a dynamic sales force at Southern Progress Corporation. He toasted the flagship's 25th with (from left) Publisher Bud Flora, Gary McCalla, and John Logue.

Jericho: The South Beheld, written by James Dickey and illustrated by artist Hubert Shuptrine, that was successfully promoted in a major feature story in *Southern Living*. By the end of the decade, the book company had landed on a perennial best seller, *Southern Living Annual Recipes*, and other highly profitable books.

From 1966 to 1978, advertising revenue in *Southern Living* grew from $600,000 to $18 million; the subscriber base increased from 250,000 to 1.6 million; and average pages per issue increased from 80 to well over 250. By the early eighties, the page counts sometimes pushed the magazine's bindery equipment to its limit.

At the beginning of that decade, The Progressive Farmer Company was enjoying such phenomenal growth that it changed its name to Southern Progress Corporation, a reflection of its broader vision. Then in 1985—just one year after *Southern Living* hit its record-breaking high of $41 million in ad revenue—Time Inc. purchased Southern Progress Corporation for $480 million. At the time, it was the largest purchase price ever paid for an American publishing firm. It was also the first time the New York media giant had acquired, rather than launched, major magazines.

Fueled in large part by generous profits from *Southern Living* and Oxmoor House, Southern Progress would spend the eighties and nineties exploring new ventures and expanding its stable of magazines. Despite the company's reputation for editorial quality, not all of its new titles made it. Those that did often had roots in *Southern Living*.

In 1985, Southern Progress released the first issue of an upscale home design magazine, *Southern Living Classics*, and not long after that merged it with *Southern Accents*, which was acquired the same year. *Southern Accents* magazine continued publication for over 20 years. Based on the success of the "Cooking Light" column in *Southern Living* and an Oxmoor House book by that name, *Cooking Light* magazine was launched in 1987 and became one of the most successful food magazines in the country. Also that year, Oxmoor House published *The Southern Living Cookbook*, the most comprehensive food book the company had ever produced.

The past 50 years have been an incredible journey for *Southern Living* and the South. It was the people of this region—our readers—who made that gamble back in 1966 well worth the risk. We have learned so much from each other. Maybe what the magazine has taught us all is that there is an undercurrent of shared cultural identity running beneath any regional differences we may have. Whether our roots are in North Carolina or Louisiana, it's all Southern soil. "There is a natural, emotional commonality in the South," John Logue once said. "It's undeniable. It's invisible. And we've learned not to talk about it. We learned that if something was truly Southern you never had to say it."

—Valerie Fraser Luesse

50 YEARS OF *SOUTHERN LIVING* COVERS

1966-1970

50 YEARS OF *SOUTHERN LIVING* COVERS

1971-1975

50 YEARS OF *SOUTHERN LIVING* COVERS

1985-1990

50 YEARS OF *SOUTHERN LIVING* COVERS

1980-1985

50 YEARS OF *SOUTHERN LIVING* COVERS

1975-1980

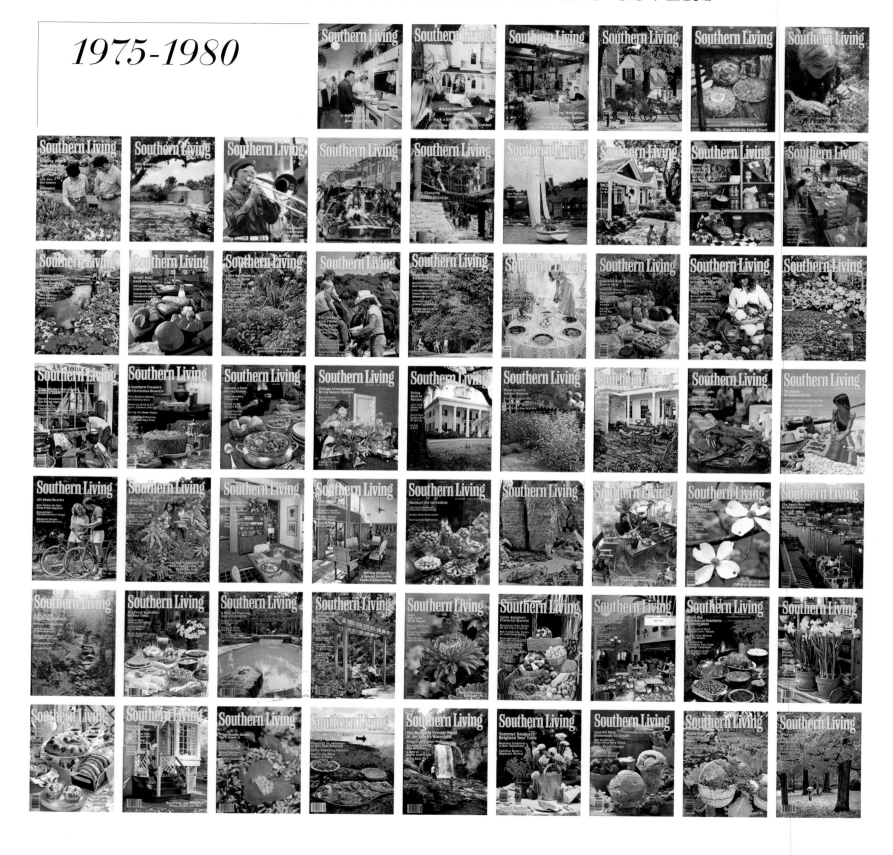

2005-2010

1990-1995

50 YEARS OF *SOUTHERN LIVING* COVERS

1995-2000

2000-2005

2010-2015

TIMELINE
—
THE PROGRESSIVE FARMER
&
Southern Living

FEBRUARY 10, 1886

Col. Leonidas L. Polk of Anson County, North Carolina, launches his weekly newspaper, *The Progressive Farmer,* to advocate for farm families. He has no way of knowing that he has just laid the cornerstone of a company whose impact on the South will be felt for generations.

1966

[February] *Southern Living* makes its debut with a circulation of 250,000, with a cover price of 25 cents. The magazine is LIFE size—and so is the reader response. *The Progressive Farmer* veteran O.B. "Cope" Copeland, much beloved in the company, is the launch Editor.

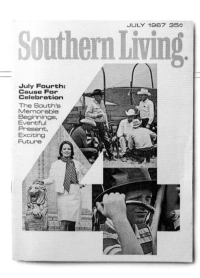

1967

[July] *Southern Living* chooses one of the smallest issues of the year to **reduce its page size**. Readers feel cheated, and the angry mail comes pouring in. The magazine begins accepting liquor advertising.

"We felt that urban people were much more liberal in their views about alcoholic evils than farm people. So our Board approved liquor advertising in S.L., provided the copy was in good taste and otherwise acceptable."

—EUGENE BUTLER

1903-1909

Clarence Poe joins with four associates to buy *The Progressive Farmer* for $7,500 and form the Agricultural Publishing Company, later renamed **The Progressive Farmer Company**. The publishers pioneer localized editorial, a model *Southern Living* would not only follow but expand, giving readers region-specific articles and enabling advertisers to target their message.

1911

The Progressive Farmer Company moves from **Raleigh, North Carolina,** to 4th Avenue North and 17th Street in **Birmingham, Alabama,** a rail hub that could streamline magazine distribution. Magazines were reportedly carted to the Birmingham post office by wheelbarrow.

1965

When publishers assemble the founding staff of *Southern Living*, they are headquartered in a **restored cotton warehouse** and fallout shelter on Birmingham's 19th Street. Dumbwaiters transport proofs up and down from the typesetting department in the basement to *The Progressive Farmer* editors above. John Logue, one of the editorial visionaries at *Southern Living*, would later describe the old headquarters as "a building out of Dickens."

1968

Emory Cunningham announces that *Southern Living* has reached its five-year **circulation goal** of 500,000 in just under two years.

1969

Gary McCalla becomes Editor.

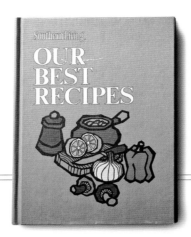

1970

An in-house book company, **Oxmoor House,** is incorporated. Its first best seller, *Southern Living: Our Best Recipes,* is released the following year.

1971

In the November issue, *Southern Living* publishes a sponsored home that was designed specifically for the magazine. It is a forerunner to the **Idea House program** that launches in 1989.

1982

The first **"Cooking Light"** column runs in *Southern Living.* Four years later, Oxmoor House publishes a book by that name, and in 1987 *Cooking Light* becomes a national magazine.

1985

ABOVE: Henry Grunwald, Editor in Chief of **Time Inc.,** celebrates the purchase of Southern Progress Corporation for $480 million.
RIGHT: Executives from **Time Inc.** and Southern Progress visit together after the sale.

"Southern Living *has become an intrinsic part of the Southern region, its people, and its unique culture. We intend to keep it that way.*"
—DON LOGAN,
CHAIRMAN AND CEO OF SOUTHERN
PROGRESS CORPORATION, 1990

1973

Southern Living reaches 1 million circulation and follows its readers to the suburbs, moving into a **new headquarters** designed to reflect the company's commitment to conservation and responsible development.

1980

The Progressive Farmer Company changes its name to **Southern Progress Corporation,** reflecting its expanding stable of magazines and books and its broadening audience.

1978

The new *The Progressive Farmer/Southern Living* **Cooking Schools** reach an audience of 200,000. Soon, the traveling cooking demo show will focus solely on *Southern Living.*

1989

Southern Living presents its first **Southern Home Awards,** honoring outstanding residential design across the region.

1989

Southern Progress Corporation moves to a **new headquarters** campus with almost 30 wooded acres on Birmingham's Lakeshore Drive.

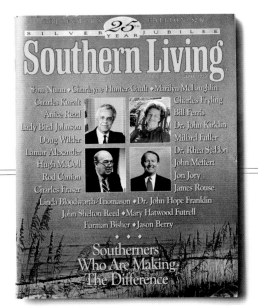

1991

Southern Living celebrates its **Silver Jubilee** with two collector's editions (January and June).

2008

Eleanor Griffin is named Editor in Chief of *Southern Living*.

2007

Progressive Farmer is acquired by DTN, a news and weather information services company.

2010

M. Lindsay Bierman becomes Editor in Chief.

2012

Three stories from the **Thanksgiving** issue are journalist finalists for the James Beard Foundation Award.

"My goal was to switch from writing so much about history and to focus on today's South—to include all middle-class Southerners in the magazine.
—JOHN FLOYD

1991

John Floyd becomes Editor in Chief of *Southern Living*.

1992

After rising to chairman and CEO of Southern Progress, **Don Logan** is named President and COO of Time Inc. He will later become chairman and CEO of Time Inc. and hold other chairmanships within parent company Time Warner. His successors as Southern Progress CEO, Jim Nelson and Tom Angelillo, will also rise through the ranks in Birmingham.

2001

The **Southern Living AT HOME** party planning business is launched and soon has over 45,000 sales consultants from every state in the union. At the time, it is the fastest growing company in direct sales history.

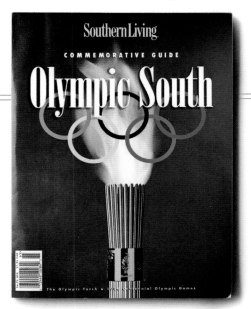

1996

As an official sponsor of the **Centennial Olympic Games** in Atlanta, *Southern Living* presents special editorial features throughout the year, including "The Road to Atlanta," which spotlights Southern athletes competing in the games.

2014

Sid Evans is named Editor in Chief of *Southern Living*, with editorial oversight of sister magazines *Cooking Light* and *Coastal Living*.

"We Southerners know how to add a little magic to everyday life. That's what this magazine has always been about."
—SID EVANS

1

JOURNEY SOUTH

Travel stories are all about the thrill

of the hunt. ◆ Over the past 50 years, *Southern Living* writers and photographers have traveled just about every highway and byway in the South, searching for picturesque little towns, great barbecue joints where the smoke drifts out to meet you in the parking lot, the next great Charleston inn, the best new restaurant in New Orleans. ◆ In the early days of the magazine, a tiny travel staff was scrambling to cover the entire South without the aid of websites, GPS technology, or cell phones. The Progressive Farmer Company had only one WATS line, so

NOVEMBER 1966 35¢

Southern Living®

They Leased
a Southern Plantation
for Hunting, Fishing

Something for Everybody

NOVEMBER 1966

Ultimately, the *Southern Living* audience would be composed mostly of women, but the magazine initially hoped to serve the whole family. Early issues included features on hunting, fishing, and other outdoor pursuits aimed at men.

35

travel editors had to get on the switchboard operator's waiting list if they needed to make a long-distance call to schedule an interview or request a photograph (which would have to be snail-mailed since nothing was digitized).

"I was probably the only travel editor they ever had who couldn't read a map," says Caleb Pirtle, who joined *Southern Living* to oversee the Travel department in 1969. It didn't matter, though, because Pirtle loved rambling his way across the South as locals encouraged him to detour here and there. From the beginning, he believed the mission of *Southern Living* Travel went far beyond hotel and restaurant recommendations. People and place are intricately intertwined in the South. A successful travel feature, Pirtle believed, needed to capture both. That meant *Southern Living* travel editors would set out to discover the South firsthand, and they would cover it as no other magazine ever had.

During the early seventies, Pirtle and photographer Gerald Crawford—both sporting the long hair and hippie garb you might expect from young journalists back then—had to find creative ways to win acceptance in the conservative small towns they frequented. "We would walk into some down-home beer joint, and the locals would look at us like they weren't sure what we were up to," he remembers. "I would walk straight across the dance floor, put in three quarters, and play three Merle Haggard songs. Suddenly, we were home folks."

Karen Lingo, Pirtle's first Assistant Travel Editor, remembers carrying stacks of *Southern Living* on trips so that she could hand them out to promote the magazine. "We all did that," she says. "*Southern Living* was not well known back then, so we would strike up a conversation with somebody sitting next to us on a plane or in an airport terminal and give them a copy of the magazine. I also took magazines to interviews because the people I had arranged to talk with usually had no clue what *Southern Living* was."

Lingo joined the magazine as a part-time Editorial Assistant in 1967. Later, having become a full-time Assistant Editor, she was earning a whopping $3,500 a year. Because the conservative Progressive Farmer Company generally didn't allow men and women to travel together unless they were married to each other, and all the photographers at the time were male, Lingo had to learn to take her own pictures.

"My first trip for *Southern Living* Travel was to Tallahassee, Florida, and I was so green it was ridiculous," Lingo recalls. "It was a press trip with five gentlemen who wouldn't allow me to pay for anything, so when I came back to Birmingham, I filed an expense report for ten dollars. Gary McCalla called me in and said, 'We are not freeloaders—when you travel for the magazine, pay your own way.' Then he padded my expense report because he said I would make everybody else look bad."

Lingo and other passionate storytellers on the staff helped define and elevate *Southern Living* Travel for decades with their in-depth research and distinctive writing styles.

Capitalizing on readers' love for sense-of-place stories, *Southern Living* was able to present powerful features on preservation and conservation. In February 1969, "Quest for the Guadalupes" took readers to this West Texas range before it became a national park. A July 1998 piece called "Miles of Memories" explored the Natchez Trace, while "Protecting Paradise" gave readers a better understanding of the South's treasured barrier islands. Even though the underlying—sometimes overt—message of stories like these was "protect the natural beauty of the South," the stunning landscapes and seascapes made readers want to go there; so as far as the audience was concerned, these features were travel stories, not environmental advocacy pieces.

Most important of all, the personal contact between readers and travel writers helped solidify a powerful bond of mutual appreciation and respect.

"We would cover small towns that no magazine had ever visited before," Pirtle explains. "And if *Southern Living* thought their town was important enough to write about, then by golly they thought the magazine was important enough to subscribe to. We might have been young and upstart, but we were a legitimate magazine. Everybody thought we were important. And after a while, we became important."

> "*Southern Living travel editors would set out to discover the South firsthand.*"

"The Mississippi Delta begins in the lobby of the Peabody Hotel in Memphis and ends on Catfish Row in Vicksburg."

—DELTA NATIVE DAVID COHN, FROM *WHERE I WAS BORN AND RAISED*, 1948

THE QUILL AND THE MULE

BY RICK BRAGG (PICTURED WITH HIS MOTHER)

In one of my most delicious daydreams, I stand at the gates of the Southern Writers' Hereafter, wondering if my name is on the list. Suddenly the gates swing open to reveal a sanctum of velvet drapes, leather chairs, and a bar lined with bottles of brown whiskey.

Scholars have long debated the defining element of great Southern literature. Is it a sense of place? Fealty to lost causes? A struggle to transcend the boundaries of class and race? No.

According to the experts, it's all about a mule. And not just any old mule—only the dead ones count. Ask the experts. I have written two dead mules into two books. That's how I know I am bona fide.

Southern writers were killing mules even before Faulkner drowned a perfectly good team in the Yoknapatawpha River in *As I Lay Dying* in 1930. The carnage has been written about in *The Southern Literary Journal* and debated at academic conferences.

In modern-day literature, new whippersnappers who wouldn't know a mule from a hole in the ground are killing mules by the caravan.

I grew up on stories of noble mules. The mule meant survival for my grandparents in the 1930s. I hate to see the hardworking beasts herded off cliffs. Then again, I can cast no stones. In my first mule story, my Uncle Jimbo won a bet by eating a sandwich while sitting on one.

SOUTHERN WRITERS tell the stories of our region like no one else can. Here are just a few of the many great regional writers who have been featured in *Southern Living* over the past five decades.

Fannie Flagg

Pat Conroy

James Dickey

Maya Angelou

Kathryn Stockett

Reynolds Price

Harper Lee

Winston Groom

Mark Childress

DEEP SOUTH

---

*The soul of the region
can be found only by
exploring the Bible Belt.*

Seven Chimneys Farm
CLARKSDALE, MISSISSIPPI

Blues giant Muddy Waters grew up in a shack that once stood on Stovall Plantation. Today, the remains of Waters' shack are displayed at the nearby Delta Blues Museum—but you can stay in a shack or an Airstream at Seven Chimneys Farm, once part of the storied plantation.

SOME PLACES LOOK COMPLETELY DIFFERENT
up close. Cross the Mississippi on a bridge high above the muddy
water and you can see the breadth of the river but not its force. You
can't judge its depth or feel its powerful undercurrents. The same
is true of the Deep South, most often defined as the band of five
states stretching from South Carolina across Georgia, Alabama,
and Mississippi to Louisiana. Collectively, they have been called
the Cotton States, the Buckle of the Bible Belt, and the Cradle of

Civil Rights. But to appreciate them fully, you have to step closer—walk the furrows of a cotton field, drive the Blues Highway, pass the offering plate, make a roux, and watch enough college football to predict who will take the SEC championship every year.

There's a lot to take in. So it's no surprise that this is some of the most fertile creative ground in America. It's the birthplace of Cajun music, zydeco, and Delta blues, the "blue-eyed soul" of Muscle Shoals, and the hip-swiveling rock-and-roll of a former truck driver named Elvis. The Deep South has produced a slew of renowned writers, artists, and craftspeople.

Southern Living was also born here. Perhaps more than any other part of the region, the Deep South sparked the idea for the new magazine. This many-layered slice of the South was once covered with cotton, sugarcane, and rice fields. By the late fifties, leaders of The Progressive Farmer Company didn't need demographic studies to point out the great shift from farms to cities, because they could see it happening all around them. Likewise, they didn't need the evening news to tell them that the Civil Rights Movement was changing the social fabric of the South, because the struggle was unfolding in their neighborhood.

Because *Southern Living* was launched from the epicenter of a great transformation, the editors would come to understand the tension between old and new, between the desire for change and the resistance to it. And the Deep South found in *Southern Living* a magazine that would look beneath the surface and mark its depths.

Cahaba Lilies

BIRMINGHAM, ALABAMA

The endangered shoals lily is native to South Carolina, Georgia, and Alabama, where the Cahaba River hosts the largest known stand of them.

"I went to New York during the 1960s, and it was very hurtful to me for people not to realize what Birmingham was really like."

—FANNIE FLAGG, *SOUTHERN LIVING*, NOVEMBER 2010

The Shoals
FLORENCE, ALABAMA

Brittany Howard and Alabama Shakes are part of a new generation of Southern musicians achieving worldwide fame. The Athens, Alabama, natives deliver a unique blend of roots rock, soul, and rhythm and blues with shades of the legendary "Muscle Shoals sound" created by FAME and other Shoals-area studios during the sixties and seventies.

Poor Monkey Lounge

MERIGOLD, MISSISSIPPI

Willie Seaberry, aka Po'
Monkey, drives a tractor
farming the fields by day and
plays juke-joint godfather
on Thursday nights at his
address-less lounge located
off US 61.

Ground Zero

CLARKSDALE, MISSISSIPPI

With most of the old juke joints gone, Oscar-winner Morgan Freeman and his business partners opened this hot spot in 2001 to support authentic Delta blues musicians.

Gee's Bend Quilts

BOYKIN, ALABAMA

Necessity bred creativity in a Black Belt community on the Alabama River, where a group of local women have kept African-American quilting traditions alive for generations. They celebrate the annual airing of the quilts where they hang them on the clothesline as an unspoken way to share them with neighbors.

THE QUILTS OF GEE'S BEND

The Gee's Bend quilts are "eye-poppingly gorgeous," declared *The New York Times* art critic Michael Kimmelman, who hailed them as "some of the most miraculous works of modern art America has produced."

> *"Everyone, rich or poor, deserves a shelter for the soul."*
>
> —SAMUEL MOCKBEE, ARCHITECT & CO-FOUNDER, RURAL STUDIO

Rural Studio

HALE COUNTY, ALABAMA

Samuel "Sambo" Mockbee believed in teaching his students as much about social responsibility as architecture, while designing inspirational homes—like this corrugated cardboard pod house—for the people of the Black Belt community.

The Grove

OXFORD, MISSISSIPPI

Cheerleaders rally the crowd
on college football game day.

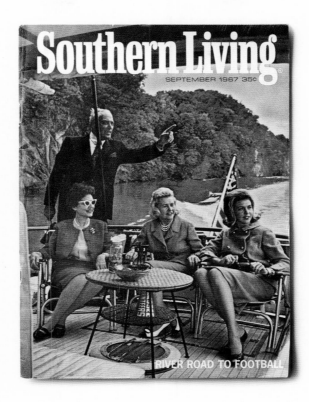

A SOUTHERN TAILGATE

In October 1966, *Southern Living* introduced readers to a party genre that seemed tailor-made for a region where food and football are equally revered. "It's called tailgating," the magazine announced, "and it is a happy blending of two pleasant ingredients, footballing and picnicking."

Fans would choose a spot, spread blankets on the ground, and lower the tailgate—of their station wagons—to break out the cooler of fried chicken and potato salad, and catch up with old friends. (Absent a station wagon, *Southern Living* pronounced it acceptable to pop the trunk.)

While tailgating had not yet become the cultural phenomenon that it is today, it was already popular in the late sixties. Ole Miss fans were gathering at the Grove, while Bama had the Quadrangle and Tennessee fans started riding boats on the Tennessee River (pictured above) to the waterside stadium in a flotilla that's known as the Vol Navy. Today, the pregame picnic has become such an important part of the whole football experience that some schools have carefully orchestrated tailgate plans and guidelines.

Back in 1966, *Southern Living* pointed out that, while Southerners have

no exclusive on tailgating, they can enjoy it longer "in light-jacketed or shirt-sleeved comfort" while Big Ten fans are "shivering beneath their topcoats and laprobes." The editors also locked into the lasting appeal of the tailgate, namely that it gives fans something to look forward to even when the outlook for their team is grim. As *Southern Living* put it then, "The popularity of the party takes some of the pain out of the pounding the home team takes." We might not make it to the Sugar Bowl, but as long as the pimiento cheese is good, we'll get somehow through the season.

On a sylvan knoll above Carter Stadium in Raleigh, a football family has lunch break.

The Colors of Fall
Are the Colors of Football

Winter. Spring. Summer. Are all seasons of discontent. You may have read it, or you already knew: that 10 Saturdays make a year.

Fall without leaves you might imagine. Fall without college football would be a "bare ruined choir" of indifference.

The colors of the game—the colors against colors—are as much of the game as the scores. The colors on these pages are the white and red of North Carolina State versus the orange and purple of Clemson. Clemson carried the day last season, 24-19. But it was State that went on to win the championship of the Atlantic Coast Conference.

It is a great series that has decided the Atlantic Coast title five of the last seven years.

As the colors of college football roll back on these pages with the first days of September, we are also prepared with

Left—*Cathy Moss rings down the pep and pizzaz so necessary for the firing up of her Clemson Tiger team in its ritual game with Atlantic Coast rival North Carolina State.* **Right**—*North Carolina State defenders give a literal interpretation of "Hold That Tiger," putting the sudden stop on Clemson's all-South fullback of 1968, Buddy Gore.* Photographs by Bruce Roberts

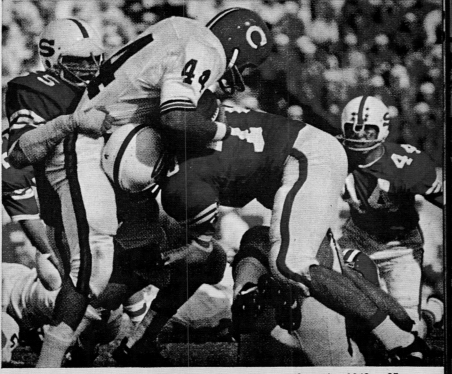

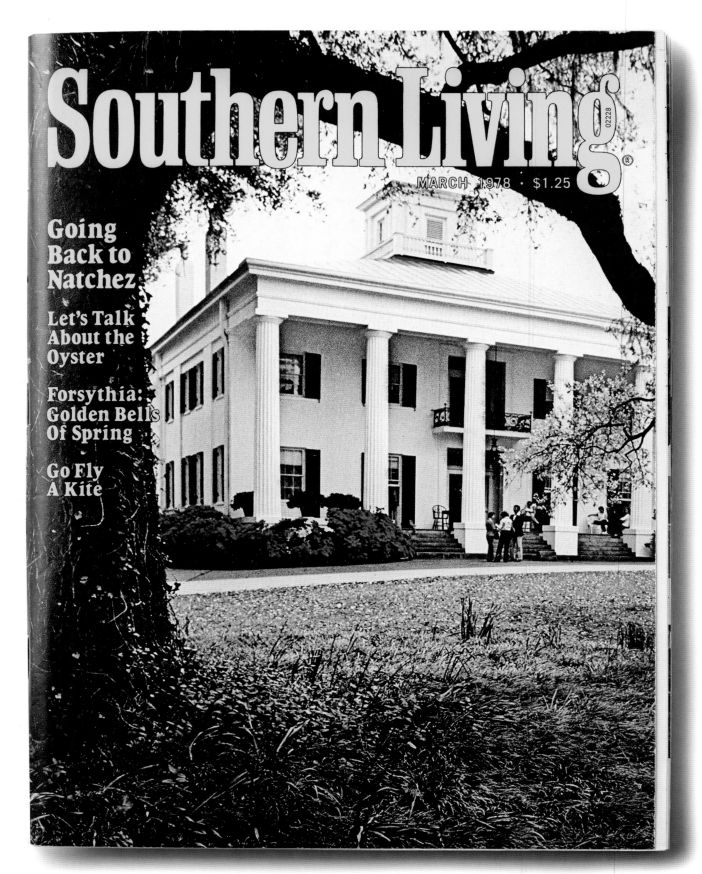

Southern Living

MARCH 1978 · $1.25

Going Back to Natchez

Let's Talk About the Oyster

Forsythia: Golden Bells Of Spring

Go Fly A Kite

Going Back to Natchez

MARCH 1978

Old homes like D'Evereux, built in 1840, have helped Natchez, Mississippi, preserve its architectural heritage. This issue had extensive coverage of one of the largest pilgrimages in the South.

MARCH 1966 — 25¢

Southern Living

AN EDITION OF THE PROGRESSIVE FARMER

Vacation on the Mississippi's Delta Queen
Best Southern Lawn Grasses

Delta Queen

MARCH 1966

Coverage of the Mississippi River traces back to the beginning of the magazine. There's something about floating down the middle of the broad river from Memphis to New Orleans that can take you back to the era of Mark Twain.

"We've got a new church with a baptismal pool, but we still go to the lake. I'll still be going to the lake till I get too old."

—REVEREND EDGAR MARSHALL, *SOUTHERN LIVING*, OCTOBER 2009

My Mississippi Delta

BY JULIA REED

AUTHOR OF *BUT MAMA ALWAYS PUT VODKA IN HER SANGRIA!*

WHEN I FIRST LEFT MY HOMETOWN OF GREENVILLE, MISSISSIPPI, the heart of the region known as the Mississippi Delta, I headed north, first to Washington, D.C., and then to Manhattan. Coming back for a visit always meant flying into Memphis, where, in those days, it was possible to connect to the 25-minute flight that took you straight into Greenville. But I almost always chose to make the two-and-a-half-hour drive instead. After even a short time away, the Delta was (and still is) a destination that demands a reentry of sorts, like when an astronaut learns to adapt to terra firma after far too many days of weightless living. For me, it meant renting the biggest car I could find and heading south on Highway 61, where midway over that last "hill" the sign says "Welcome to Mississippi" and I'm entering what feels like a dome turned on its side. Almost immediately, the light's different (the only other place I've encountered it is in Tanzania's Ngoro Ngoro crater) and that familiar scent of chemicals mixed with ancient earth—far more evocative than a whole box of Proust's madeleines—floods the car as soon as I roll down the window. Then there are the signs marking the towns as I blow by—Hollywood, Lula, Rena Lara, Alligator—playing like reassuring mantras in my head. At some point I cut over to the old road that more closely hugs the river, Mississippi Number One, immortalized by my friend the great blues pianist Eden Brent in her song (and album) of the same name. When she sings "there ain't nothing but a two-lane highway between me and my childhood home," I'm right there with her, passing the abandoned gas station near Gunnison where a tame deer used to smoke—and swallow—a cigarette, driving too fast through Beulah where a promised pecan pie from Greenville's Sherman's Grocery once rendered my speeding tickets moot, stopping at the White Front Café in Rosedale for the first of many Delta tamales. Finally, just past the Indian Mounds, built more than 1,000 years ago by the Delta's first settlers, the sign says Greenville, and once again, I'm home.

Even now, almost four decades after I first left at sixteen to go off to boarding school, I still respond "the Mississippi Delta" whenever anyone asks me where I'm from. And then, almost invariably, I have to explain exactly what it is that I mean by the term. Usually, I make like a first-grade teacher and hold my forefingers and thumbs in front of my face in the shape of a diamond. "This is Memphis," I say, tapping my fingers together at the top. "Down here where my thumbs meet is Vicksburg, on my right is the Yazoo River, and here in the middle, on the Mississippi, is Greenville." I repeat what Greenville-born writer David Cohn said about the Delta beginning in the lobby of the Peabody Hotel and ending on Catfish Row in Vicksburg. I tell about the ducks that swim in the Peabody's marble lobby fountain, descendants of live decoys left there by Delta hunters in the 1930s, and explain that Memphis is our spiritual capital, "a place," wrote Peter Taylor in his brilliant last novel *A Summons to Memphis*, "of steamboats and cotton gins, of card playing and hotel society."

Next, I point out that what we mean by "the Delta" is not the actual river delta at the mouth of the Mississippi, but an ancient alluvial flood plain some 300 miles north.

I tell them that not only is "our Delta" 7,000 square miles of some of the richest land in the world, but it was pretty much uninhabitable until well into the 1820s when a handful of folks rich enough and crazy enough turned up to literally hack it out of an oft-flooded hardwood forest chock full of panthers and mosquitoes and snakes. More than anything, I say, the Delta gives lie to the idea of the monolithic South, or even a monolithic Mississippi. And if I'm really on my game, I quote Shelby Foote, the novelist and Civil War historian who was also from Greenville: "The first thing you have to understand is that all this business about moonlight, magnolias and Anglo-Saxon bloodlines has to go out the window. The Delta is a great melting pot."

Foote, whose maternal grandfather was a Viennese Jew who at one time owned a plantation, told an interviewer, "I was perfectly aware that there was a world outside because my grandfather came from that world." And that was the thing. The Delta has always comprised a cosmopolitan mix of born travelers who'd arrived on the scene from places as far-flung as Kentucky and South Carolina, Russia and Austria, Syria and Cantonese China for economic opportunity and left their significant imprint on the culture. And early on, there was considerable traveling to be done within the Delta itself. Those early planters were forced to GO long distances over rough terrain just to socialize with one another— house parties and road trips were the order of the day, and old habits, apparently, die hard. In the Delta I grew up in, no one thought twice about jumping in the car to make the two-hour-plus trek to Memphis in time for dinner at the late great Justine's.

These days, when I go back—I head north from my current base in New Orleans. On that route, reentry begins just after Vicksburg, where the bluffs give way to that familiar wide flat landscape. I make a traditional beer stop at the Onward Store and take a left at Highway 14. Then I'm back on Number One, singing along with Eden on "the last of the bluest highways" along "miles and miles of sandy loam." I listen to her words and realize that what I should say to the folks who ask is that the Delta is a great gift, from the river itself of course, but also from all those who carved it out and worked it afterwards in conditions so insufferable it gave us the blues. It is also entirely inseparable from who I am.

"The Delta was (and still is) a destination that demanded a reentry of sorts . . ."

——

Soulsville USA

MEMPHIS, TENNESSEE

A banker and his sister created Stax Records and moved it to the old Capitol Theater in 1960. Soon they would record the likes of Otis Redding, the Staple Singers, Sam and Dave, and Isaac Hayes, with Booker T. & the MG's as their longtime house band.

Dolly Parton

NASHVILLE, TENNESSEE

In January 1971, Parton was the lone girl singer featured in a major piece on "the men who make the Nashville sound a $100 million-a-year industry." Today, she is an industry unto herself.

"I've always been proud of who I was and of my people. I'm proud of where I'm from."

—DOLLY PARTON, *SOUTHERN LIVING*, SEPTEMBER 2014

COUNTRY MUSIC

From its storytelling traditions in the 1920s rural South to today's cross section of pop, country music has had a huge influence over the region. Here are a few more of the female stars who have appeared in *Southern Living*.

Martina McBride

Kimberly Schlapman

Emmylou Harris

Valerie June

Speaking Up for Atlanta—Finally

BY JOHN HUEY

FORMER EDITOR IN CHIEF OF TIME INC. AND BONA FIDE ATLANTAN

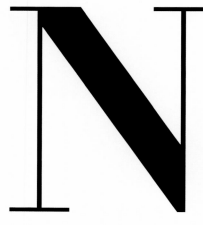

ot in my wildest dreams did I imagine I would ever ask such a question, but isn't it time someone spoke up on behalf of Atlanta?

Back in 1987, a New Yorker writing for *The Wall Street Journal* described Atlanta as "an archipelago of shopping malls and condominiums with an atrophied downtown, snarled traffic and a fading sense of community." As a native, I should've taken offense at this description, but, in fact, I was the journalist's editor at the time, and I applauded his acuity in grasping the essence of my hometown.

Now, entirely to my surprise, after roaming the world for 40 years, I've had a change of heart. I have come to realize the city has just been misunderstood.

Yes, Atlanta is a mess. But you might be too if you were a rickety little railroad town of fewer than 10,000 folks that was sacked at the end of the Civil War, then rebuilt rather quickly into a megalopolis with an area the size of Massachusetts and a population double that of Mississippi.

And yes, everyone prefers my adopted hometown of Charleston—with its meticulously preserved historic architecture, ancient mossy live oaks, and acclaimed culinary culture. But Charleston is a very old place. Founded in 1663 and built on the backs of slave labor, it was the richest city in North America at the time of the American Revolution. Atlanta? It wasn't even legal for white people to live where it sits until 1821, when the Creek Indian nation ceded it to the state of Georgia. Charleston bears the regal name of England's King Charles II; Atlanta is a coined word, a fake brand name like, say, "Lunesta," slapped on it by a Yankee railroad promoter in 1845.

No port. No beach. No mineral wealth. No *there* there. But Sherman was on to something when he burned it to the ground. He could see clearly that it was already becoming a vital transportation hub. And that was a plan Atlanta was happy to run with as it quickly grew from a burnt-out husk of a town into a burgeoning city crisscrossed with railroads.

Something else important happened in the aftermath of the Civil War, as carpetbaggers from up North poured into the boomtown. John D. Rockefeller came south and adopted the cause of educating the former slaves. He backed Spelman College (named for his wife's family), which would one day count among its graduates both the grandmother and mother of Dr. Martin Luther King, Jr. He also adopted fledgling Morehouse College, which taught generations of black professionals, including such esteemed leaders as W.E.B. Du Bois, Julian Bond, and the Nobel Prize-winning Dr. King himself.

Almost a century later, this effort reaped huge rewards for the city, and the country, as Atlanta became the Southern oasis for both the leaders of the Civil Rights Movement and the national press covering this profound American struggle. Since then, it has been the mecca for African Americans returning to their Southern roots, and for aspiring black entrepreneurs. I once asked entertainment mogul Tyler Perry why he left his native New Orleans for Atlanta instead of New York or L.A. He responded: "Because I visited relatives here when I was a kid. It was the first time I'd seen so many black people living in nice houses and driving nice cars. I couldn't wait to get here."

While much of the rest of the South turned inward well into the 20th century, Atlanta was as open as a Quickie Mart and remains so today. Coca-Cola, Home Depot, and CNN were all born there. Giants like UPS moved there. Today it boasts the busiest airport and the largest airline—Delta—in the world.

In the 1970s, when Jimmy Carter deregulated the airlines, breaking the stranglehold that a handful of cities had on travel to Europe and Asia, Atlanta's international trade exploded. Immigrants from all over the world flooded in, bringing with them all manner of exotic products, customs, and foods. The strip malls of Chamblee, near the old Naval Air Base, became known as "Chambodia." The Dekalb Farmers Market popped up and has become one of the most amazing cornucopias of global foodstuffs in the world. In Gwinnett County, where we camped in cow pastures as Boy Scouts, the malls today feature acclaimed Korean food.

For all that, Atlanta never wins any style points. Getting from where it started to where it is today just wasn't as pretty as everyone might have wanted.

I am happy to report, though, that yet another new Atlanta is growing up in the shadows of the city most people see while passing through. This new Atlanta is authentic and fresh and energetic but has managed to restore some ties to its ephemeral history.

The Beltline, for example, is a 22-mile greenway linking 45 neighborhoods on old railroad rightaways; it finally gives Atlantans an enjoyable way to get out of their cars and feel their city on foot or bicycle. The once provincial little town of Decatur has become a hot spot for music clubs, ambitious restaurants, and an amazingly audacious cocktail culture exemplified by the Kimball House, set in the old railroad station near Agnes Scott College.

And, with multiple chefs anointed by the James Beard Foundation, Atlanta is now fully participating in this whole gush of romanticism over Southern cuisine. Anne Quatrano's Bacchanalia, Linton Hopkins' Restaurant Eugene, and Hugh Acheson's Empire State South led the way. Steven Satterfield of Savannah has reinvented "comfort food" at Miller Union, in the long-overlooked but architecturally appealing old meatpacking district. These hot spots aren't pretenders; they are seriously good.

After dinner one night around the corner from Miller Union at the distinctively reimagined Star Provision complex, I was walking across the footbridge that spans the Norfolk Southern Railroad tracks when I had a moment. Two lengthy freight trains were passing under the bridge in opposite directions—one leaving Atlanta for points west, the other headed into the nearby freight yards. If you grew up here—especially in the open-window days before air conditioning—the sound of these trains rumbling across the city all night long is what you remember, and maybe miss the most, about Atlanta. It was comforting that night, but somehow exhilarating, to realize that the little old railroad town is still working away down there somewhere under the formless glitz.

What was that feeling washing over me? Could it have been *pride*?

"*I have come to realize the city has just been misunderstood.*"

APPALACHIA

—

These mountains have a story to tell, from the origins of bluegrass to the birth of the Southern craft movement.

Pisgah National Forest

WESTERN NORTH CAROLINA

When Biltmore creator George Vanderbilt died, his widow honored his lifelong commitment to forestry by selling 86,000 acres of the estate to the federal government, establishing a National Forest.

COLD, CLEAR STREAMS rushing over moss rock, dense forests and wildflowers, white-tailed deer and the American black bear—they're all part of the daily scene in Appalachia. And when fall paints the peaks and valleys with brilliant color, the rolling landscape is illuminated with countless shades of red, orange, and gold, shadowed in evergreen. Here, nature makes dramatic statements, from West Virginia's New River Gorge to the serene

sweep of the Shenandoah Valley, described by *Southern Living* writer Les Thomas in March 1998 as "a place of stunning beauty, rimmed by the Blue Ridge, laced with tumbling streams, and spread with a quilt of farms and lovely towns."

Carving out a place for themselves in this vast wilderness, the people who made their home in Appalachia—English, Irish, Scotch, and African-American settlers, as well as Native American tribes—carried with them rich traditions of music, storytelling, and crafting, passed down for centuries. Whittlers and fiddlers, painters and potters, singers, dancers, writers, and quilters—not to mention *Southern Living* writers and photographers—have all put their creative energy to the task of capturing the beauty and mystery of this place.

It is remarkable not only for what's here but also for what has come from here. Many early greats of American racing inadvertently prepared themselves for Daytona, Charlotte, and Darlington by running moonshine in Appalachia. And the same densely wooded mountains that cloaked the stills have in-spired generations of artisans, drinking in the breathtaking scenery like a 90-proof elixir. From

glassblowers to wood-carvers, the Appalachian craftspeople have long expressed themselves in ways that are deeply rooted in place—in the shapes, forms, and colors of their surroundings. You can see it in places like Asheville, North Carolina; Berea, Kentucky; and the thriving arts community surrounding North Carolina's renowned Penland School of Crafts.

Then, of course, there's the magic of fiddle, guitar, and banjo. Once Virginia natives A.P., Sara, and Maybelle Carter stepped up to the microphone, country music had its First Family. Their audience would later be expanded exponentially by yet another daughter of the mountains, Dolly Parton. In the 1940s, when two talented guys named Flatt and Scruggs joined Kentuckian Bill Monroe and his Blue Grass Boys, "high lonesome" bluegrass was born.

Perhaps the ultimate gift of the Appalachian South is that it calls us to celebrate what is authentic and timeless. We are profoundly moved by the splendor of the mountains, by the ancient ballads of lost love and broken hearts, by things of beauty made by skilled hands, by the Carters' "roses so red and the lilies so fair," and the memory of that "pale wildwood flower."

OCTOBER 1966 35¢

Southern Living®

FOLLOWING
THE FOLIAGE TRAIL
IN THE
GREAT SMOKIES

The Leaf Crowd

OCTOBER 1966

Before RVs and SUVs, pickup trucks with camper shells caravanned through the Smokies. Gary McCalla, future Editor of *Southern Living*, followed the foliage seekers on an October Sunday when an early morning snow had capped the autumn-lit mountains "like whipped cream on top of a giant fruit salad."

71

A view along the Appalachian Trail near Clingman's Dome.

Five Great Hiking Trails

Each one a winding mountain path through nature's November spectacle

The flush of autumn foliage now blazes across the countryside. There is a perfect way you can see it. Hike up into the mountains and through the trees.

Not since the days of the raw frontier have so many Americans sought out places to walk quietly through the native beauty of the land. And nowhere in America are there more outstanding hiking trails waiting to be enjoyed than in the Southeast and Southwest.

The most spectacular fall scenery is in the mountains. Here are five memorable trails that you can hike, either seriously or casually with the entire family.

JOYCE KILMER MEMORIAL FOREST—One of the most impressive remnants of our nation's virgin wilderness lies in the Joyce Kilmer Memorial Forest.

This 3,800-acre forest is a living memorial to the author of *Trees*. It is in the heart of the Nantahala National Forest in extreme western North Carolina. The forest contains some of the largest virgin timber still growing on the North American Continent and is a spectacular combination of huge hardwoods and evergreens, some of which are hundreds of years old.

To reach Joyce Kilmer, you turn off U.S. 129 just north of Robbinsville, North Carolina, onto a graveled Forest Service road that runs for 6 miles. The road is narrow and twisting and somewhat rough. But you can make the journey in OK with your car.

The Joyce Kilmer Forest is reserved for serious nature lovers who are willing to experience some small inconvenience to get there.

From the small oval parking lot, just inside the forest boundary, you can begin hikes that vary in length from several hundred yards to several miles.

The shortest hike takes less than an hour and is easy for the entire family, small fry included. This walk, which is marked, leads through the largest trees in the forest—giant yellow poplars and hemlocks, many 20 feet around at the base and well over 100 feet tall. Many deciduous trees contrast their flaming foliage against the greens of the hemlocks, pines, laurel, and rhododendron.

Sycamores, basswood, dogwoods, beech, oaks, and gum grow in abundance.

If you wish to spend more than a day exploring the depths of Joyce Kilmer Forest, bring your camping gear and warm clothing and settle down in the Horse Cove Recreation Area, just outside the forest.

Here you can camp alongside either Little Santeetlah or Big Santeetlah

Creeks, both good rainbow and brown trout streams. You might also want to bring a canoe or cartop boat and spend some time fishing in Lake Santeetlah, just downstream.

If you wish to devote several days to hiking, you can explore much of the 21-mile trail system in Joyce Kilmer, working your way up from your campsite at 2,400 feet to such points as Jenkins Meadow, Haoe Overlook, and Stratton Bald, at well over 4,000-foot elevations.

In addition to ancient trees, you will see a remarkable variety of smaller mountain flora. You may also see deer, bear, wild boar, fox, bobcat, raccoon, skunk, squirrel, mink, weasel—or ruffed grouse, wild turkey, ravens, and various owls and hawks.

This visit to one of the few remaining American forests undisturbed by man, whether of short or fairly long duration, will be hard to forget.

THE APPALACHIAN TRAIL FROM NEWFOUND GAP TO FONTANA DAM—The Appalachian Trail, which extends 2,000 miles from Spring-er Mountain, Georgia, to Mount Katahdin in the northern Maine wilderness, is the longest continuous marked trail in the world. One of its most challenging, but also most scenic, portions is the 37-mile stretch between Newfound Gap and Fontana Dam in the western North Carolina Great Smokies.

Most of these 37 miles are definitely for the more practiced, hardier hikers. Clingman's Dome (6,642 feet), the highest peak in the Smokies and on the whole Appalachian Trail, is on this section of the trail, as are Silers Bald, Thunderhead, Shuckstack, and other steeply sloping mountains. But the impressive views from these mountaintops will compensate adequately for your exertion. It is wise to plan on at least 3 days for this hike, and, depending on the weather, perhaps 4. There are 10 trail shelters, each with wire bunks, at convenient intervals along the way for rest stops and overnight camping.

Newfound Gap, your starting point, is 15 miles from Gatlinburg, Tennessee, on U.S. 441 and 26 miles from Bryson City, North Carolina, on U.S. 19 and 441.

The trail is well marked with white paint blazes, standard Appalachian Trail markers, and cairns. Intersections are marked with board direction signs, and side and major approach trails are marked with blue paint blazes.

The trail at Newfound Gap begins on the northwest end of the parking area where you descend through an opening in the guard wall onto a graded trail which parallels a Park Service road.

Continuing straight ahead for about a mile, you will ascend to the crest of Mount Mingus Ridge. You will be able to see Mount LeConte through the balsam trees to your right. At the crest, bear left and descend the ridge until you come to Indian Gap. The slopes of the gap are cleared because during periods of heavy snow it is used as a ski run. Ascending again for 3 miles, you will reach the summit of Mount Collins (6,188 feet). There are fine views south as you descend steeply to Mount Collins Gap.

About 2 miles farther on you will reach the summit of Mount Love, then

Autumn in Virginia

OCTOBER 1967

Celebrating Virginia's hunt country and the Blue Ridge, this early cover story took readers on a driving tour that included a stop at the Boar's Head Inn, where hotel rates—$165 and up these days—started at $14 per night.

Southern Living

OCTOBER 1967 35¢

Enchanting Autumn in Virginia
Acres of Roses, Texas-Style
The Many Roles of Cornmeal

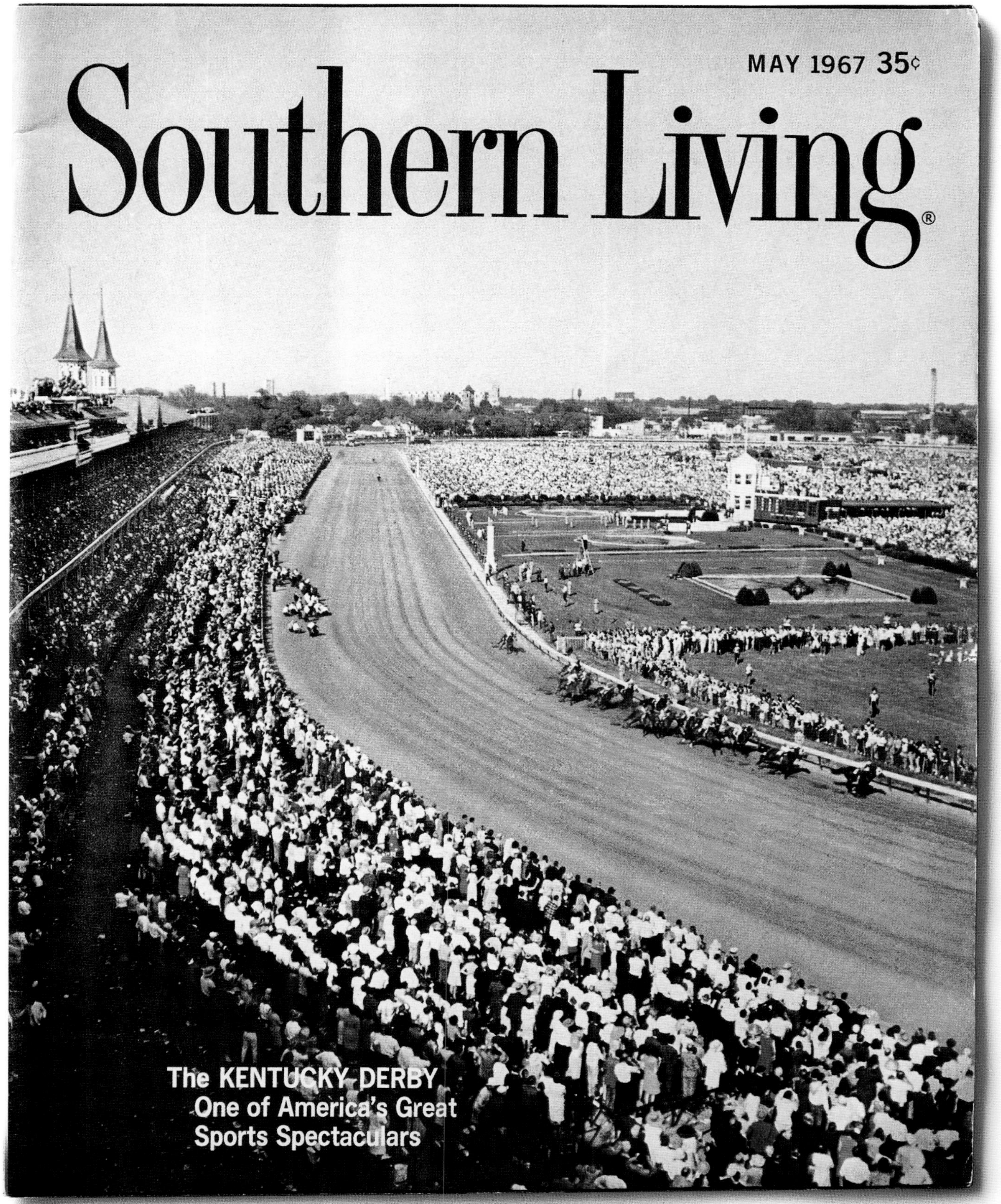
MAY 1967 35¢
Southern Living®
The KENTUCKY DERBY
One of America's Great
Sports Spectaculars

A LOOK BACK

Run for the Roses

MAY 1967

With the fashionable hats and mint juleps, the parties, parades, and "My Old Kentucky Home," the release of the starting gate is an anticlimax, *Southern Living* pointed out in this colorful trip to Churchill Downs.

Churchill Downs

LOUISVILLE, KENTUCKY

The Kentucky Derby is all about the hats, which have been making a statement here since 1875, when Southern race-goers adopted a tradition of their English counterparts.

Buffalo Trace Distillery

FRANKFORT, KENTUCKY

Distilleries dot some of the prettiest countryside in the South and have created such signature brands as Maker's Mark, Jim Beam, and Pappy Van Winkle. A few distilleries were even allowed to produce "medicinal" bourbon during Prohibition.

Barboursville Vineyards

BARBOURSVILLE, VIRGINIA

Pioneering Italian vintner Gianni
Zonin helped spark the rebirth
of Virginia winemaking when
he purchased the Barboursville
Vineyards near Charlottesville
in 1976. Today, the state has a
thriving wine industry covering
nine wine regions.

Virginia's oldest hunt club was founded in 1896, but foxhunting was part of the sporting scene here as early as 1742. The hounds sometimes take their morning exercise at neighboring Keswick Hall.

THE SOUTHWEST

—

Our own big sky country sweeps across some of the most spectacular terrain in America.

Rio Grande River

BIG BEND NATIONAL PARK, TEXAS

Beginning with a convergence of streams in Colorado, the "big river" flows almost 2,000 miles to the Gulf, forming a natural boundary with Mexico and cutting a dramatic path through the sheer limestone walls of Santa Elena Canyon.

WHILE IT'S A MISCONCEPTION to think the whole of the Southwest looks like a scene from a classic Western, the rugged reaches of this area have a way of capturing our imaginations. Craggy mountain ranges like the Davis, the Chisos, and the Guadalupe rise out of the flatlands, while such fabled waterways as the Red River and the Rio Grande have carved extraordinary canyons out of the Texas Panhandle and the Big Bend. Contrasting with this cowboy topography are the Piney Woods of East Texas, Oklahoma's Tallgrass Prairie, and the Ozark Mountains.

Southwest cityscapes are equally varied, with colorful small towns, such as Eureka Springs, Arkansas, and Fredericksburg, Texas; thriving arts communities in Oklahoma City and Tulsa; and cosmopolitan metro areas like Houston and Dallas, which are not only national hubs for business and travel but major cultural centers.

One of the earliest *Southern Living* fan letters came from a Dallas resident who praised the debut issue but wanted to make sure the editors got Texas right—particularly his native East Texas, which more closely resembles Mississippi than El Paso. "There isn't a tumbleweed nor a prairie dog for literally hundreds of miles!" he wrote. He was also aghast that so few people knew about Austin, "the 212,000-population capital of Texas!" (That figure has since risen past the 800,000 mark.)

Southern Living entrusted the Southwest to writers and photographers who not only understood and appreciated it but also could interpret it for the uninitiated. Such talented journalists as Dianne Young, Gary Ford, Tanner Latham, and Les Thomas explored the Southwest for decades, crisscrossing it with photographers Mark Sandlin, Gary Clark, Art Meripol, Laurey Glenn, Ralph Anderson, and Robbie Caponetto. They conveyed a sense of awe for the place and a genuine connection with the locals. In an April 2005 feature, Young describes the "spare beauty and the mighty stillness" of the Chihuahuan Desert, where "clouds, fired by light and ripped by wind, streak across an improbably blue sky." Such a landscape makes a lasting impression, lingering with you even if you must one day return to the "real world" and leave these wide-open spaces behind.

Bluebonnets

MASON, TEXAS

Like magic, it appears and then
vanishes—a fleeting show of
spring wildflowers that paints
the whole countryside in
brilliant shades of blue.

Southern Living

JANUARY 1979 · $1.50

Rafting the
Rio Grande

Living Above
The Store

Twigs Can
Be Beautiful

Brighten
Your Menus
With Citrus

The Future of
The South: The Land
A Special Section

Made by the River

JANUARY 1979

Cradled by a bend in the Rio Grande, Big Bend National Park occupies 800,000 acres, with river, desert, and mountain habitats. In 1979, *Southern Living* described the park's Santa Elena Canyon as "a veritable stone box holding a river within its grasp for 10 winding miles."

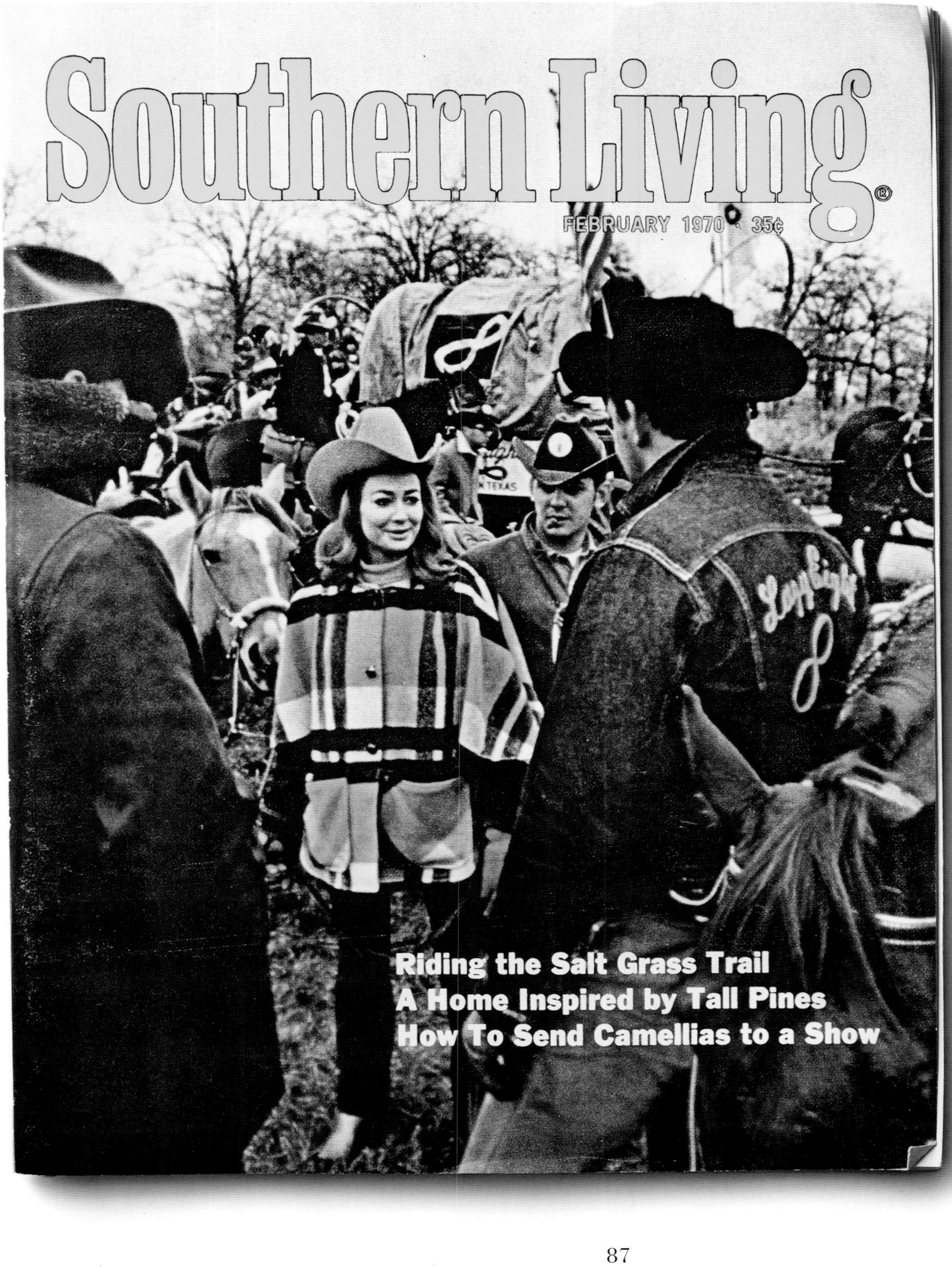
Southern Living
FEBRUARY 1970 · 35¢
Riding the Salt Grass Trail
A Home Inspired by Tall Pines
How To Send Camellias to a Show

A LOOK BACK

City Slicker

FEBRUARY 1970

Southern Living travel writers have tried everything from zip lining to scuba diving. For this cover story, then-Features Editor John Logue and photographer Gerald Crawford saddled up for the 95-mile Salt Grass Trail from Brenham, Texas, to Houston.

Medina River

SOUTH CENTRAL TEXAS

On hot summer days, Hill Country rivers attract paddlers and tubers eager to escape the heat. While the Guadalupe is the most popular, the less-crowded Medina meanders under the welcome shade of bald cypress trees.

BEST LITTLE HONKY-TONK IN TEXAS

James and Annetta White's Broken Spoke on South Lamar in Austin remains little changed since it opened its doors back in 1964 (when beer set you back a quarter), though the city itself has grown up around the little red board-and-batten dance hall.

Today the Lone Star capital is known as much for its high-tech industry and South by Southwest festival as it is for weirdness and Texas Longhorns. Once inside the honky-tonk walls, lined with cowboy hats from famous folks like Willie Nelson, LBJ, and George Strait, new and old Austin come together as urban cowboys and Daisy Duke wannabes, real-life ranchers and square dancing housewives move in a united two-step across the dance floor to live country band music that's been the draw five nights a week for over fifty years.

Such is the scene in dance halls across Texas where you can catch up on live music or even take dancing lessons. These are special spots found throughout the region where the music is honored and beer and whiskey are plentiful.

Anhalt Dance Hall

SPRING BRANCH, TEXAS

Kicker dancing is alive and well at country places like this, where directions to the venue read "follow the road to the very end and cross the cattle guard to the gate on the left."

San Antonio
Renaissance on the River

*Once abused and ticketed for a bed in oblivion,
the San Antonio River is now a "moveable feast" of flowers and trees and shops.
Today it not only flows, it swings.*

by H. M. MASON, JR.

I am a lover of cities tied together by rivers.

As a youth I was fortunate enough to share in that "moveable feast," Paris, and it was the broad and gentle Seine that so often provided a million francs' worth of deep and lasting pleasure when there was a not a sou in the pocket.

Much of that enjoyment has, over the years, been looted from Parisians. The areas at river level where the weight lifters, the acrobats, and the chalk painters used to perform have mostly been given over to concrete ramp access lanes jammed with minicars traveling noisily at maxi speeds. It is a pity; when the demands of the internal combustion engine are met at the sacrifice of open areas intended for people—to work, to love, to play, to contemplate—the loss is bitter and irrevocable.

Cities in the world that were built along the banks of a river because the place was beautiful, and not because the water offered commercial promise, are rare indeed. San Antonio is one of these cities, and one of the great pleasures of living here is to choose a fine cool spring day and amble along the banks of the river, leaving traffic and downtown office buildings 20 feet above your head. The place surrounds you with native greenery of every configuration: heavy-leaved oleander, straight-up cottonwood (*álamo*, the Spanish called it), dagger-like palmetto, a great and ancient oak with one massive branch stretching horizontally from one bank to the other, geometric shapes of thick-laced carpet-

Left—*With HemisFair's Tower of the Americas behind them, children ride a pedal boat down the river.* **Right**—*Outdoor dining is featured at El Palicio del Rio.*
Photographs: Gil Barrera

Thanks to a terrific food and music scene, together with lakes and bike trails that make the most of its Hill Country setting, the state capital has become one of the most popular cities in the South.

Riscky's Steakhouse

FORT WORTH, TEXAS

A walk through "Cowtown" is like a blast from the past in the Texas city that mixes small-town charm with metropolitan edge.

Southern Living

AUGUST 1976 · $1.00

Oklahoma Spotlights
An Indian Powwow

Homemade Peach Ice Cream

**Southern Plains
Native Americans**

AUGUST 1976

Native American contributions
to the arts and culture of the
South cannot be overstated.
In Oklahoma, which is home
to many tribes and languages,
Native American art is
central to the holdings of
fine art museums such as
the Philbrook in Tulsa.

State Fair

DALLAS, TEXAS

The same downtown event that features a 212-foot Ferris wheel and a 52-foot mascot named Big Tex has become famous for deep-fried everything: Chicken Fried Bacon, Deep Fried Butter, Fried Thanksgiving Dinner—all this, plus one of the biggest games of the college football season between Texas and Oklahoma, played at the Cotton Bowl stadium during the fair.

Gravel bar camping is the mainstay of overnight camping trips on the Buffalo. Sites are clean, and an air mattress ensures sound sleep.

Born Free
The Buffalo National River

This wild and free-flowing river in the Arkansas Ozarks has been saved as a haven for canoeing, hiking, and camping.

by TOM ADKINSON

There's something peculiar about the Buffalo River in northwest Arkansas—at least by Arkansas standards.

That something peculiar is something precious few rivers in the United States enjoy: From its source in the Boston Mountains to its end almost 150 miles away, the river never once is stopped by a dam.

It is no small accomplishment.

The winding, free-flowing Buffalo cuts through rugged country. Back in geo-

Arkansas' Buffalo National River widens in its lower stretches for relaxed canoeing.
Photographs: Joe Benton

logic history, the area was a plateau, but the river and other streams carved it into ribbons of ridges. It doesn't hold much natural wealth. Some lead and zinc have been mined in years past. Timber operations decimated certain tracts. The soil is rocky and not very productive. Not many people live here.

You might assume the land is as good as any to inundate. It would be easy to tame this slashing and deceptively powerful river with a dam or two, the way most Arkansas rivers are controlled. In fact, there were plans for just that: one dam on the lower stretch and another more toward the middle near Gilbert.

Suddenly, the dam builders had a

fight on their hands, and eventually the river won. It is to remain free to prowl the Arkansas Ozarks. What saved it was a simple change of names. Instead of being the Buffalo River and subject to all kinds of tampering, it now is the Buffalo National River and is permanently protected from any kind of interference. It is a project of the National Park Service.

A spaghetti-strand of federal land is being born along 132 miles of the river from around Boxley to near Buffalo City. The Buffalo's upper reaches lie inside the Ozark National Forest. More than 95,000 acres ultimately are proposed for the national river property,

COASTAL
SOUTH

—

*Pristine beaches, serene marshlands,
and cypress-lined bayous skirt the
Southern shoreline.*

Scenic 30A
FLORIDA PANHANDLE

A Gulf-hugging highway meanders through some beautifully designed communities, including Seaside, Watercolor, Rosemary Beach, and Alys Beach, all fronting miles of spectacular white sand.

THE SOUTH HAS ITS SHARE OF "BEACH PEOPLE."
Our affinity for the coast is understandable, given that 11 of the
17 states within *Southern Living* territory touch saltwater. We
are mesmerized not just by the sheer scope of the Southern
coastline—almost 36,000 miles of it, including tidal areas—
but also by its tremendous geographic and cultural diversity.

The stark natural beauty of Cape Hatteras on
North Carolina's Outer Banks is worlds away
from the marshlands of the Lowcountry or the
shag-dancing frivolity of Myrtle Beach to the
south. Within Florida alone lies the Panhandle,
a mecca for family beachgoers; the hard-packed,
hard-driving sands of Daytona, where NASCAR
was born; the Everglades; and the funky, bohemian
Conch Republic of Key West. Head farther west
and the sugar-white sands of Alabama's popular
coastline give way to the flat waters and live oaks
of coastal Mississippi, followed by Louisiana's
eerily beautiful bayou country and Texas' Padre
Island and Laguna Madre.

Our connection to the coast is visceral. Former
Southern Living Senior Writer Les Thomas

captured it in a June 2007 piece on Hampton Roads,
Virginia, which he described as "America's
waterfront": "It's the smell of salt air rising off the
Chesapeake Bay and the snap of sails billowing
on the masts of a tall ship. It's the way a sailor hugs
his family when he's finally home from sea. It's
the fragile boats of Jamestown settlers, the
thunder of the *Monitor* and the *Merrimack*, and
the rattle of liberty ships sailing bravely for
far-off shores."

The coast has a way of luring us like no place
else. Every walk on the beach makes us long for
another one. Every sunset has to be the most
glorious one we've ever seen. We might return
in a month or a year, but this much is certain:
We'll be back.

Southern Living

MARCH 1973 · 50¢

The Southern Seacoast ...

Coastal Preservation

MARCH 1973

In the early seventies, planned development was relatively new in the South, but states were beginning to recognize the need for coastal land management. *Southern Living* stressed the importance of protecting the water, sand dunes, and tidal zones, and spotlighted seaside communities that were getting it right, such as Amelia Island Plantation near Jacksonville, Florida.

American Classic

TYBEE ISLAND, GEORGIA

The more developed our beaches become, the more we appreciate authentic coastal villages that know how to take it easy. Relaxed and bike-friendly, historic Tybee is only 18 miles from Savannah.

Coast Guards

APRIL 1989

Seven of America's ten National Seashores are in the South, including Cape Hatteras, featured on this 1989 cover. The magazine encouraged readers to experience these singular stretches of coastline firsthand and, perhaps as a result, help protect them.

"The best oysters in the country grow plump and sweet on Southern tides."

—HUNTER LEWIS, FORMER EXECUTIVE EDITOR, *SOUTHERN LIVING*, JANUARY 2015

Southern Living

MARCH 1982 · $1.95

Fishermen of
The Southern Coast

Remembering St. Augustine

Small Houses Live Big

Don't Overlook
The Minor Bulbs

Breakfasts &
Brunches

SWELLY NAN

CAPT. CLYDE

Fish Tales

MARCH 1982

Two years before author Mark Childress published his first novel, he wrote a day-in-the-life feature that followed Southern fishermen from the Chesapeake Bay to Texas, where this cover was photographed at Sabine Pass.

Cape Point

HATTERAS ISLAND, NORTH CAROLINA

The barrier islands of the Outer Banks weather fierce winds and tides but deliver breathtaking natural beauty. Their treacherous shoals have sunk countless ships, prompting mariners to name them "the graveyard of the Atlantic."

"*A fisherman hates to obey another man, but he always obeys the sea.*"

—MARK CHILDRESS, AUTHOR AND FORMER FEATURES WRITER, *SOUTHERN LIVING*, MARCH 1982

Wadmalaw Island

CHARLESTON COUNTY,
SOUTH CAROLINA

A chain of more than 100 Sea Islands
extends along the coasts of South
Carolina, Georgia, and Florida.
On Wadmalaw Island, the
Charleston Tea Plantation
produces American Classic Tea.

Main Street

BEAUFORT, SOUTH CAROLINA

The best small towns in the South offer historic architecture, thriving main streets, pedestrian-friendly neighborhoods, and front-porch views. Upping the ante, coastal communities such as Beaufort throw in live oaks with Spanish moss draped like Christmas tinsel.

Southern Living®

APRIL 1970 · 35¢

Charleston's Journey Through Three Centuries

Charleston, South Carolina

APRIL 1970

The historic downtown, romantic courtyards, and coastal character of Charleston have always held a special appeal for *Southern Living* readers. Even those who have never set foot on King Street have a vision of what this great Southern city must be like.

Savannah, Georgia

MAY 1972

Having survived fires, wars, and epidemics, Savannah almost surrendered to what *Southern Living* called "a parking lot future" in the first half of the 20th century. But then a grassroots effort in the fifties led to the Historic Savannah Foundation, which promoted restoration and changed the city's course for good.

SCAD

SAVANNAH, GEORGIA

Magnolia Hall at the Savannah College of Art and Design (SCAD) overlooks historic Forsyth Park. Founded in 1978, SCAD is internationally renowned, offering 40 areas of concentration—from graphic design and painting to writing, performing arts, and historic preservation.

The French Quarter

NEW ORLEANS, LOUISIANA

Even a powerful hurricane like Katrina couldn't shut off the lights in the Quarter forever. In 2013, eight years after the storm, New Orleans hosted more than nine million visitors, who spent $6.47 billion—the city's highest spending level ever.

Antoine's

NEW ORLEANS, LOUISIANA

If jazz didn't exist,
the food alone would be
reason enough to love the
French Quarter. Some of its
venerable restaurants,
such as Antoine's, have been
run by the same families
for generations.

Grayton Beach

FLORIDA PANHANDLE

Only the sugary sand
and distinct waters of
this quirky little beach
community are more
popular than its famed
Red Bar. Grayton accurately
touts itself as "an eclectic
beach burg," with an artsy
bent that keeps it interesting.

The Gulf

ORANGE BEACH, ALABAMA

For years, Gulf Shores and neighboring Orange Beach were small villages with mom-and-pop motor courts and a smattering of restaurants. Development boomed, however, after Hurricane Frederic in 1979, bringing condos, chain hotels, and lots of family-friendly entertainment.

Southern Living

OCTOBER 1970 · 35¢

The Beaches of October

Beach Bargains

OCTOBER 1970

Back when low-tech RVs were popular, campsites were part of the draw for places like South Padre Island, Texas. *Southern Living* recommended the 18 camp cabins at Isla Blanca Park, where vacationers could sleep six for $8.24 a night (but bath facilities were next door).

2

WELCOME HOME

So many aspects of Southern life

that seem commonplace today were just beginning to emerge in 1966. ◆ Suburbs were a relatively new phenomenon in a region that had, throughout the 19th century, remained much more rural and less affluent than other parts of the country. ◆ *"Southern Living* and the modern South really came into their own together," explains Philip Morris, who joined the magazine as Building Editor in 1969. "A generation earlier, this magazine never would have happened because there weren't enough people here who could have lived that suburban lifestyle." ◆ Southern metro areas

AUGUST 1966 25¢

Southern Living®

Outdoor Living

AUGUST 1966

This St. Petersburg, Florida, home illustrated the growing Southern trend to let the outdoors in, which makes landscaping and lighting more important. The feature states, "More people are finding they can enjoy added living space far into the night with a few well-placed light fixtures."

like Atlanta and Dallas-Fort Worth were rapidly expanding, and most cities had yet to see how profoundly the choices they were making, all in the name of progress, could affect their long-term health and livability. "Preservation was a real frontier then," Morris says. "I think what *Southern Living* did on that front was really important to the South because we were hitting it at a time when so many cities could have gone either way. We just found examples of preservation done well and conveyed that it should be part of what we do as a culture."

Accustomed as they are to seeing design professionals featured in *Southern Living* and other magazines, contemporary readers are at least acquainted with the design world, maybe even comfortable in it. But in the sixties and seventies, most Southern homeowners had no idea what a landscape architect did or how dramatically a well-designed landscape could enhance their homes. Even though the South generally gravitated toward traditional architecture, *Southern Living* helped them recognize *why* they liked what they liked by showcasing the best traditional design in the region. In the process, Morris would "move *Southern Living* away from featuring 'pretty'" and begin giving readers a broader design perspective, says former Editor in Chief John Floyd, who brought an equally strong design focus to the Garden department when he joined the magazine as editor of that section in 1977.

What evolved into the *Southern Living* look in homes and gardens was driven, to a large degree, by the magazine's decision to use staff writers and photographers. These "boots on the ground" provided constant personal contact with Southern families, which kept the magazine firmly rooted in the South and gave it an honest picture of how readers lived. That was critical because the editors believed they needed to reflect both the aspirations and the realities of their audience.

In the beginning, the magazine leaned heavily on practical, problem-solving editorial and didn't cover home interiors extensively.

"Southern Living *and the modern South really came into their own together.*"

—

But by the early seventies, the editors had recognized the broad appeal of interior design stories and began looking for designers who embraced the magazine's solution-based philosophy.

The Garden department, as much as any other section, educated readers and inspired them to explore new terrain. *Southern Living* showed readers how to downsize the farmstead vegetable garden to a suburban scale and put a Southern spin on the Western concept of indoor-outdoor living that was so popular with *Sunset* readers. Screened porches, breezeways, decks, pools, and terraces became staples of the magazine. Fall gardening wasn't popular in the South until *Southern Living* promoted it with an annual fall pansy feature. "When we first started, our supplier was growing about 100 flats of pansies a year," Floyd recalls. "Three years later, he sold 20,000 flats."

Since the launch of *Southern Living*, so much of the magazine's strength has come from the community it has built—not just a network but a true community—of the South's best architects, master builders, landscape architects, and interior designers. *Southern Living* has a long history of celebrating their work and using it to inform and inspire readers. Renowned architect Frank McCall, whose work included a number of projects on Sea Island, Georgia, had never been published when *Southern Living* first met with him. Yale alumnus James L. Strickland, founder of Historical Concepts in Atlanta, credits the magazine with putting his firm on the map. It has created numerous *Southern Living* Idea Houses and house plans, and has won multiple Southern Home Awards from the magazine. "I see *Southern Living* today embracing the future, as well as the past, of Southern architecture and featuring designs that are a little more cutting edge," Strickland said. "Over the years, the magazine has continued to present a great study of architecture, of what makes a wonderful home and environment. That's an extraordinary contribution to the South."

SOUTHERN LIVING IDEA HOUSES

Southern Living readers have never been completely satisfied just to read about beautiful homes and gardens—they want to step inside them. In fact, many of them dream of owning a home or garden that looks "just like *Southern Living*."

The November 1971 issue featured "A House Designed for *Southern Living*." With the American Wood Council as a sponsor, the magazine presented the same house in Memphis, Houston, Atlanta, and Charlotte, opening all four to the public. These were

forerunners of the *Southern Living* Idea House, launched in the January 1989 issue with "The Twin Gables," designed by Stephen Fuller, Inc., and built north of Atlanta. Today, the magazine collaborates with national sponsors and a design team to create two Idea Houses each year, open for tours and featured in the August issue.

Back in the seventies, the editors saw an opportunity when they discovered that readers were contacting the owners of featured homes. Working with some of

the South's best residential architects, the magazine launched a monthly "House Plans." *Southern Living* House Plans, published in the fall of 1987, became the first special-interest magazine from *Southern Living*.

Today, *Southern Living* offers over 1,000 house plans featuring the work of more than 150 architects, as well as a Custom Builder Network and Design Network. Together, these services make it possible for a reader to create a home designed for living in the South.

THE SOUTHERN FARMHOUSE

—

What's not to love about a house that's simple, functional, and connected to the land.

Moss Mountain Farm

ROLAND, ARKANSAS

Wedded to the land that sustains it, a classic farmhouse offers the simplicity of traditional rural homes, combined with modern comforts.

ONE OF THE MOST POWERFUL FORCES that shaped *Southern Living*—one that made the magazine not just possible but necessary—was a postwar population shift away from struggling farms and into flourishing suburbs. In recent years, *Southern Living* has seen a reversal of that trend, at least in spirit. Readers in the cities and suburbs have a renewed interest in their agrarian roots and in the architectural forms of an era when life moved to slower, less complicated rhythms.

Farmhouse architecture captures that simplicity with an uncluttered, highly functional design. Windows are placed to maximize natural light and promote breezes, while covered porches tie indoor living spaces to the outdoors. Once a shady locale for shelling and shucking, the porch was also a prime spot for visiting with neighbors, a tradition that lives on in the South.

Our desire to revisit the farm goes beyond the house itself. Today, you will find citified chicken coops in suburban backyards across the South, and we've raised backyard vegetable gardening to an art form. Canning has made a comeback as a new generation discovers the satisfaction of "living off the land," even if we define that as growing a few patio tomatoes or a container herb garden.

The lasting appeal of a farmhouse is that it makes us feel as if we've come Home with a capital "H," that we've not only created an inviting haven for our families but have somehow reconnected with the past, with that part of ourselves that is very much of the South. Most of us won't be returning to those long-ago farmsteads, but we respect what they represent—family, memory, and the indelible bond between a plot of land and the people who tend it.

Screening Room
Southerners use porches, like this one at Moss Mountain Farm, for everything from dining to serious napping. In the summertime, porch screens offer protection from the unofficial mascot of hot weather, the mosquito.

Charleston Green
According to legend, when Union soldiers sent buckets of paint to help rebuild Charleston, South Carolina, residents couldn't abide the government-issue black and tinted it with green and yellow. This greenish black "Charleston Green" remains a favorite for shutters and other architectural accents at Moss Mountain Farm and all across the South.

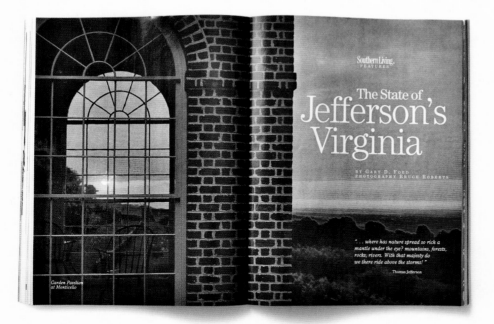

Garden Pavilion at Monticello

MONTICELLO

Monticello has long been a source of pride in the South. In the April 1993 *Southern Living*, former Senior Writer Gary Ford highlighted the intellectual and artistic breadth of its creator: "Thomas Jefferson was first a jurist and then an architect, a horticulturist, a philosopher, a farmer. He was a writer, a viticulturist, an archaeologist, a mathematician, a meteorologist. He was a pretty good fiddler, too."

Jefferson designed Monticello, his iconic neoclassical Virginia home. Though the original structure was completed in 1784, Jefferson would expand and improve upon it throughout his lifetime.

"Its grounds served as one of the young nation's first true experimental farms," wrote Steve Bender in the September 2012 issue. "A 1,000-foot-long vegetable garden, terraced by hand into a red clay hillside, embodied the Slow Food ethic nearly two centuries before it became a movement. Today, this garden inspires a new generation of gardeners to preserve locally adapted selections of vegetables and fruits to enrich our diets and promote genetic diversity."

Because Jefferson placed his vegetable garden on an elevated terrace facing south, he enjoyed a year-round harvest and made what Bender calls "his biggest contribution to the Southern dinner table": hot-weather vegetables. Most gardens focused on cool-weather crops favored by Northern Europe. Monticello was unique in introducing such heat lovers as lima beans, squash, okra, eggplant, sweet potatoes, peanuts, and the all-important tomato, which Northern Europe shunned in Jefferson's day.

The South can thank Jefferson, not only for an historic architectural treasure but also for the foods that make our summertime tables the stuff of legend.

"We may feel closer to Jefferson's heart in his garden than anywhere else on earth."

—GARY D. FORD, FORMER SENIOR WRITER, *SOUTHERN LIVING*, APRIL 1993

Monticello.
CHARLOTTESVILLE, VIRGINIA

The vegetable garden and its iconic pavilion welcome the morning's first sun.

Set amid an apple orchard, this country-style farmhouse easily adapts to the active family that built it. Rambling and rustic, the house is as spacious as its setting.

The kitchen, at one end of the greatroom, utilizes rafters to display a collection of baskets. Across the back wall hang antique cast-iron pans still used for making cornbread.

A cozy dormer bedroom has an Early American poplar rope-strung bed and comb-back Windsor chair. The wallpaper repeats an antique stenciled pattern in navy and cream.

Photographs: Mac Jamieson

Family Life-Style Produces Tennessee Farmhouse

Here is a rambling country home that breathes the friendliness of its owners and the loving care that went into its construction. It is a special place for a special way of living.

by CAROLE ENGLE

Warmth and hospitality. This new version of a traditional country farmhouse has both. Built by owners John and Mary Rankin, the house and the Rankins' life-style bespeak the Southern values traditionally placed on family gatherings and relaxed living.

"We wanted a place for our children and grandchildren to visit often," comments Mary. "That called for plenty of space both inside and out."

Nestled on top of Signal Mountain, Tennessee (near Chattanooga), the rambling frame house lodges comfortably in its spacious setting. Groves of apple and pecan trees surround the house. In character with both setting and house, a split-rail fence separates the driveway from the front yard.

The heart of the house is a 24- x 28-foot greatroom complete with kitchen. Located at one end of the house, the greatroom has its own porch and outside entrance.

From the exterior, this part of the house looks like the original structure with the larger wing added later. The house appears to have been built over a period of years instead of months—a throwback to rural vernacular ar-

A large, open greatroom is the hub of activity. Aglow with the warmth of wood, the room resembles the inside of a log cabin with exposed beams and a hearth used for cooking.

October 1978 **121**

A LOOK BACK

Signal Mountain, Tennessee

OCTOBER 1978

Southerners are enamored of old home places and even love new homes that look old. *Southern Living* has featured many residences, such as this farmhouse, which appear to have evolved over the years. The magazine would eventually develop house plans with this "added on" look.

Slate Hill Farm
CHARLOTTESVILLE, VIRGINIA

A farmhouse celebrates the landscape, with porches to encourage outdoor living and banks of windows to welcome breezes, light, and views.

"I love the simple elegance and classic order of the Virginia farmhouse."

—BETHANY PUOPOLO, ARCHITECT AND HOMEOWNER, *SOUTHERN LIVING*, FEBRUARY 2013

"DIXIE CHICKENS"

BY STEVE BENDER

Have a seat, Fido. Step aside, Furball. A challenger to your posts as the South's favorite pets is quickly moving up in the pecking order. For while dogs may fetch and cats may hunt, this critter boasts a talent neither can match: It lays delicious eggs.

Yes, the once-humble chicken is conquering new territory from Texas and Oklahoma to the Carolinas and Virginia. No longer relegated to the farm, backyard chickens are now the rage in cities and burbs, including areas so tony the butlers have servants. It seems like almost every major town boasts a poultry group, in which people from all walks of life gather to talk about raising chickens. Coop tours such as the Funky Chicken Coop Tour (held each April in Austin, Texas) and the Tour D'Coop (held each May in Raleigh, North Carolina) showcase coops ranging from the simple to the sublime.

Why is the South so taken with chickens? The motivation is clear: The appetite for locally grown food produced by people you know using methods you approve of grows stronger every day. You can't get more local than chickens in your backyard.

Living with any kind of livestock, including chickens, means keeping them safe from predators. Chicken coops need strong defenses, but that doesn't mean they have to be graceless bunkers. Surrounding them with lush climbing vines and colorful annuals helps them fit into a garden setting.

Southern Chicks

ATLANTA: GEORGIA

Nestled into a well-designed
garden, chicken coops have
come a long way from tin
roofs and chicken wire.

HOME PLACES

—

Southern roots run deep where a house and land are passed down through generations.

Carloftis Home Place
LIVINGSTON, KENTUCKY

The quintessential Southern
family home is a place of
warmth, comfort, kinship,
and shared memory.

DRIVE THROUGH THE RURAL SOUTH and you will see them—old family homes so beautifully wed to the countryside that you cannot envision one without the other. It's as if the walls, roof, and porch were not so much built on this ground as coaxed from it. Even if you knew nothing of its history and just happened by on an afternoon ramble, you could sense that this place has stories to tell, that it has lived a life and has every intention of continuing on.

Home places have as much to do with what we feel as what we see. They have the power to tie one generation to the next, bound together by the collective memory of a family. They are the scene of many celebrations—Christmas dinners and Fourth of July barbecues, birthday parties and bridal teas. They welcome us and shelter us, reminding us of who we are and where we came from.

Such a place can have a second chapter, as new stewards step in to replace those who came before, reviving the gardens and restoring the house. If no house remains and a new one must be built, it will likely be called upon to mirror what once was. We want the echo of footsteps on wood floors and the *whap* of a screened door in the summertime, the cool relief of cross breezes through windows wide open and the creak of a well-trodden stair step.

Whether handed down or adopted, carefully preserved or dutifully re-created, home places represent the most personal form of historic preservation. They give us a deep sense of kinship to a singular time and place. And they remind us, every day, of the difference between a house and a home.

Naturally Formal
In the Carloftis vegetable garden, clipped boxwoods and yews surround a weather vane, blending formal structure with rustic style.

At the Carloftis home place, Senior Writer Steve Bender described the sunlit morning mist as "a wake-up call from God."

"You're never too old to come home.
I still have my room."

JON CARLOFTIS, GARDEN DESIGNER, *SOUTHERN LIVING*, JUNE 2012

The asymmetrical window arrangement is a hallmark of early plantation plain houses, such as this Georgia home built between 1799 and 1801.

The Plantation Plain

Moved to an idyllic site and saved from the ravages of time, this plain-style, Georgia plantation house again extends hospitality to family and friends.

by LINDA HALLAM / photography JOHN O'HAGAN

A new gazebo provides a pleasant spot for outdoor dining.

When the South was wilderness to tame, early planters built sturdy two-story, one-room-deep houses adapted from the British Isles. Constructed of heart pine and other native materials, these un- pretentious houses symbolized landed wealth and gentility from Tidewater Virginia through Alabama and Geor-

Washington, Georgia, brick mason Joe Charping rebuilt the two original chimneys and added two new ones for the rear addition.

gia. The plain-style houses became the typical plantation home at a time when only the richest landowners built in the more lavish Greek Revival style.

Though later builders adapted the wide central hall of Georgian-style architecture to plantation plain houses, the earliest examples were constructed as asymmetrical-plan, four-room structures—two rooms on each floor. It is such an early house, built between 1799 and 1801 on a land grant, that Bill and Georgia Fae Leverett found to restore—and to transform into a warm and beautifully furnished country home near Thomson, Georgia.

"We had always wanted an old house and had looked for a number of years," explains Bill. "I had considered moving at least two houses prior to this one. But this house was only 3 miles from our farm, so moving it was feasible. I knew I wanted it the minute I saw it." Because the house had been held by the original builder's family, its history was easy to document.

This history and the structural strength convinced the couple that the house could be restored. "Georgia Fae and I tried to put the house back as it was prior to the modern changes," adds Bill. Acting as their own general contractor, the couple started with the exterior. "We took the asbestos siding off down to the old pine siding," Bill

continues. "I thought about saving the siding, but we needed to get in to insulate and properly plumb and wire. Since the old wood siding was in such poor condition, we came back with cypress siding and stained it."

Fortunately, the interior walls, supports, and flooring were in good condition. The original building material, heart-pine lumber, had helped the house to survive. And because the house had been cared for through the

years, such features as the pine floors, tongue-and-groove walls and ceiling, and interior doors remained intact.

With this core to work from, the Leveretts restored what they could during the 3½-year project. And they copied replacements with the help of Thomas Charping, a Washington, Georgia, carpenter. In the living and dining rooms, workmen removed plaster and paneling. The dining room's four original walls, including

(Left) *The original pine porch railing is copied in cedar. This side door leads to the dining room.* **(Right)** *New square columns duplicate the originals. Carpenters also reproduced the shutters in the style of the old ones. The porch floor is splatter-painted.*

A LOOK BACK

Thomson, Georgia

APRIL 1988

Saved from ruin and moved to a pastoral setting, this plain-style plantation home is representative of the historic preservation *Southern Living* has long celebrated and promoted. The owners saved much of the original heart pine that had given the house strength to stand for almost 200 years.

Tudor Grove

CHARLOTTESVILLE, VIRGINIA

John Singleton Mosby, "the
Gray Ghost of the Confederacy,"
spent much of his boyhood at
this historic home, lovingly
restored by Camille Price.

"An air of mystery and age enveloped this place. Aside from upgrading the mechanicals for modern convenience, I couldn't erase a thing."

—CAMILLE PRICE, HOMEOWNER, *SOUTHERN LIVING*, MARCH 2013

Lost in Time
Threatened with a golf-resort renovation, Tudor Grove was saved by owner Camille Price, who says it reminded her of an old movie set.

Aging Deliberately
Paint creatively peeled, silver allowed to tarnish, and antiques thoughtfully collected add to the character and patina of historic Tudor Grove.

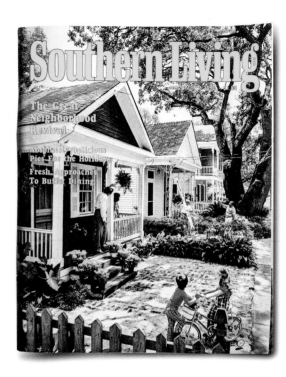

Marking the Bicentennial

NOVEMBER 1976

Southern Living celebrated America's bicentennial with a number of major features on the South and its culture, including this cover story by Philip Morris, who was Executive Editor at the time. "This is a people movement," wrote Morris, "diverse in expression but unified in the belief that old neighborhoods should not be wantonly thrown away but cared for with feeling."

Willow Oak Farm

MADISON, GEORGIA

Rooted in the rural past, this cabin
was inspired by old Southern farms
and built on family land. The wood
was repurposed from two dismantled
19th-century churches.

"It's the kind of place where you can come in from quail hunting with muddy boots and slide into a chair with a glass of whiskey."

—PHOEBE HOWARD, DESIGNER,
SOUTHERN LIVING,
SEPTEMBER 2014

Gentinetta-McAlear Cottage

NEW ORLEANS, LOUISIANA

Creole cottages, like all vernacular architecture, reflect not just the culture of the South but its climate as well.

COTTAGE HOMES & GARDENS

—

*With their simplicity
and charm, idyllic small
homes draw us in.*

COTTAGES HAVE ALWAYS held a special place in *Southern Living.* Not only do readers love cottage style, but they love the idea of a cottage life. Who among us hasn't been attracted, at one point or another, by the ease and serenity of a small house with a lovely garden?

In the best cottages, whether a shotgun or a dogtrot, a Creole cottage or a beach bungalow, perfect proportions and well-chosen details lend authenticity and a distinctively Southern sense of place. Antiques and collectibles add timeless character and charm, while modern conveniences and smart floor plans make every inch of space function well. From the style of windows and shutters to the flow of garden paths, from wall coverings to accessories, each layer of detail helps tell the story of these small gems.

But they have even more to offer than style and function. There's something about the modest size of a cottage that makes us feel self-sufficient. In a larger space, a vegetable garden might seem laborious, but change "vegetable garden" to "cottage garden" and your whole mindset is transformed. You no longer envision rows of plants that need tending but low-maintenance window boxes filled with fresh herbs, container tomatoes, and maybe a pepper plant or two.

Perhaps the lasting appeal of these homes comes from their ability to reduce design considerations to the bare essentials: How much space do we truly need, and how can we make it special? The cottage homes and gardens featured in *Southern Living* over the years have answered those questions in some intriguing ways and in all kinds of settings—beaches, lakes, and mountains; cities, small towns, and the rural countryside. Each of these homes offers undeniable proof that a small space can deliver unlimited inspiration.

Capture a Time
Even a new home, like the
Gentinetta-McAlear's (pages
162–163), modeled after an
1850 Creole cottage, can feel
authentic with the right
distressed furnishings,
patinated accessories, and
historically accurate details.

The Family Hub
Especially in small homes, many Southerners forego formal dining rooms in favor of large, eat-in kitchens like the Gentinetta-McAlear's in New Orleans.

Stanley-Seymour House

DAUFUSKIE ISLAND, SOUTH CAROLINA

A porch swing stands in for a sofa on
the back screened porch, which takes
advantage of the natural beauty of
the landscape and provides the
perfect spot for relaxing.

ODE TO THE SCREENED PORCH

BY ALLISON GLOCK

Screened porches are like tree houses for grown-ups. A semiprivate refuge that feels at once part of the world and yet separate. A comfortable perch from which to watch life amble by, to become a contented observer, to savor what is sweet and good and safe about home.

Raised in Jacksonville, Florida, I did not grow up with a screened porch. We had what was called a "Florida room," basically a tiled patio enclosed with windows in place of screens. Instead of the unmistakable whine of a screened door, my sisters and I were raised with the thunderous slam of a weatherproofed one. Mercifully, my relatives in West Virginia and North Carolina were lucky enough to have screened porches, where they did what one should do on a screened porch—smoked and told stories.

It wasn't until I was 21 that I got my own screened porch, the only winning feature on an otherwise tragic box of an apartment. No matter, it was where I spent all my hours, with my dog Sadie snoozing at my feet. As I sat there in my metal chair, listening to the cicadas, the sky bleeding blue to black, a breeze stirring the pages of my book, I felt connected— not just to my family and those days spent on their porches, but also to the bigger family of the South and to our hard-won tradition of stopping to take note.

Ingram Residence

BIRMINGHAM, ALABAMA

Small spaces allow for creative takes on the front lawn, such as a parterre garden that eliminates it altogether.

"The house is only 27 feet wide. It's no issue walking around the parterre garden, and it adds a bit of green around the front door."

—BILL INGRAM, ARCHITECT AND HOMEOWNER, *SOUTHERN LIVING*, MARCH 2013

171

Porch House

TEXAS HILL COUNTRY

With its ingenious use of
natural airflow, the traditional
Southern dogtrot continues
to inspire regional architects.

Climate Controlled
Dogtrots, like the Porch Houses in Texas, are ideal for indoor-outdoor living in hot climates, thanks to a central covered breezeway.

> *"The modern dogtrot provides something that's familiar and distinctive. It's a combination of the old and new, but not in a contrived and artificial way."*
>
> —BILL AYLOR, ARCHITECT, *SOUTHERN LIVING*, FEBRUARY 2013

Ladew Gardener's Cottage

MONKTON, MARYLAND

The loose design and layering of black-eyed Susan, coleus, and sweet potato vine give this Southern cottage garden a sense of wildness.

Clay Residence

OKLAHOMA CITY, OKLAHOMA

A tiny house requires
that the garden live large,
expanding space as it offers
indoor-outdoor possibilities.

1708

WATERFRONT LIVING

*The soothing sounds
and spectacular views enhance
our sense of escape at water's edge.*

Berard Residence

LAKE HARDING, GEORGIA

As a family's life together evolves, what once was a weekend getaway can become a permanent home, fostering a new, more relaxing lifestyle.

A Lively Design
for
A Lively Family

Bordering the golf course of a Louisiana commuter community, this home was built to accommodate the diverse interests of a family of five active people.

Covington, Louisiana, is a growing retreat for people who want to live amid quiet and calm, yet be within commuting distance of cosmopolitan New Orleans. Only 24 causeway miles across Lake Pontchartrain from the city, Covington is becoming noted for its convenient location and its handsome homes.

One of the most striking examples is the Donald W. Durant home. A family devoted to sports (particularly golf and swimming), the Durants bought a 4½-acre lot bordering the Covington Country Club—a location that would afford them convenient access to golf, tennis, and swimming. William I. Ricciuti, AIA, of New Orleans, obliged them with a uniquely designed home that almost lets them live in the outdoors.

Overall, the home embraces nearly 3,000 square feet, not including the 400-square-foot carport. The game room and living-dining area which open onto an adjacent terrace and pool dominate one side of the home. In the other wing are the master bedroom and

bath and bedrooms and baths for the three children.

The home is dramatic, bold in form and line, yet is delightfully warm and invigorating — an action home for this very active family. Easy maintenance keeps the home ready for frequent, spontaneous entertaining. Heated floors allow Mrs. Durant and the children a favorite pastime—walking barefoot in winter. An intercom system which conveys stereo over the home's interior and to the pool and terrace is especially wired to bring bird songs into the home.

In designing a home located near the 7th hole of a golf course, the architect might be expected to use a minimum of glass. Not so with architect Ricciuti. The Durants specified a home with easy movement to and from the outside. Ricciuti explained, "I designed the home for the people who are living inside it—not for those on the outside." In the process he utilized the functional and decorative potential of wood, stone, and large expanses of glass.

The most noteworthy feature is the

In foreground of the home are a rock garden and a fishpond abundant with water lilies and goldfish. Sliding glass doors from living room and game room lead onto the terrace and pool area.

A LOOK BACK

Covington, Louisiana

JANUARY 1968

Early on, *Southern Living* looked to *Sunset* magazine for inspiration. However, the West Coast style of indoor-outdoor living—a hallmark of *Sunset*—had to be adapted for the South. This sleek, modern house featured an "intercom system" that could send music outside while bringing the sounds of nature indoors.

Nason Residence

CORAL GABLES, FLORIDA

With an expanse of lawn separating them from the main house, the pool and cabana become more of a destination.

Tubb-Weaver
Residence

SMITH LAKE, ALABAMA

A new addition can dramatically transform a simple weekend cabin, opening the home to light and views as it increases living and entertaining space.

"*A lake house makes you feel like you're a kid again. You know when you enter that you're going to enjoy yourself.*"

—RICHARD TUBB,
DESIGNER AND HOMEOWNER,
SOUTHERN LIVING, JUNE 2013

Bikini Point

PICKWICK LAKE, MISSISSIPPI

A truly special lake house can be shared and enjoyed by an entire family for generations.

"*I learned to water-ski here at Bikini Point. I want our boys to share those same experiences and my love for the South.*"

—MEG BRAFF, DESIGNER AND HOMEOWNER, *SOUTHERN LIVING*, JULY 2011

Lazy
Living on the Gulf

*Basic materials and good design borrowed from the past
combine to make the new town of Seaside.
The look is laid-back but carefully planned.*
by LOUIS JOYNER

It used to be that folks who could, went to the beach for the summer. Up and down the Southern coast, they would go to their cottages, simple structures that used the breezes to keep cool. Often the cottages would be clustered together into communities where everyone knew everyone else.

The town of Seaside, Florida, isn't an old beach community; it just feels that way. Actually, it's only about 3 years old. Right now, Seaside isn't a very big town—only a few streets and about a dozen houses are built. But then owner/ developer Robert Davis isn't in a hurry. He's taking his time and doing it right.

The homes that are there evoke memories of summers long ago and show what all of Seaside will eventually be. Picket fences define the small yards. Screened porches provide shady outdoor living areas. White curtains billow in the summer breeze. You want to stay.

There's nothing pretentious in these houses, just a sweet simplicity that recalls the days before condominiums, before air conditioning.

However, Seaside is not an exercise in nostalgia; rather, according

to Architect/Planner Andres Duany, "It is the most rational, efficient way to build." Duany and his partner, Architect Elizabeth Plater-Zyberk, both of Coconut Grove, Florida, worked with developer Davis on the town's master plan and zoning code.

The architects and the developer all have strong feelings about urban design and what a town can and should be. The master plan for Seaside is a reflection of those feelings.

The master plan is very much like the layout of a typical small town. There will be a city center with shops, offices, workshops, and even a conference center/city hall wrapped around a town square, which slopes down to the water. Residential streets will be laid out in the familiar grid pattern with a tree-lined avenue and civic plaza radiating out from the central square. "We think in terms of traditional streets

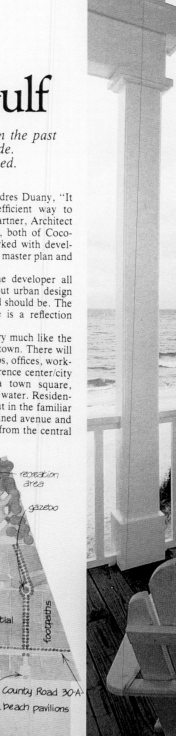

recreation area

gazebo

residential

workshops

avenue

conference center

retail

residential

residential

footpaths

square

market

TOWN OF SEASIDE MASTER PLAN

beach pavilions

County Road 30-A

beach pavilions

beach

Gulf of Mexico

*The beach pavilion (**left and below**) serves as the social focus of the street. Changing rooms flank the observation deck. When the development is completed, each street will have its own pavilion.*

(**Above**) *These houses are new, but they look like they belong in a turn-of-the-century vacation community. The unpaved street runs to the beach.*

Photographs: Louis Joyner

A wide, screened porch wrapping two sides of Robert Davis's house provides plenty of comfort. The floor is pressure-treated pine; the underside of the corrugated metal roof shows between ceiling joists.

Seaside, Florida

JUNE 1984

When then Homes Editor Louis Joyner introduced readers to this visionary community, only a few streets and about a dozen homes had been completed. The now-thriving town center was still on the drawing board. Together, Seaside and *Southern Living* changed the South's perception of what coastal development could look like.

Beachfront Residence

ROSEMARY BEACH, FLORIDA

On the Gulf of Mexico, porches
rise above the dunes to offer an
unobstructed view of the water,
which draws Southerners to
these shores like a magnet.

> *"The houses of Rosemary Beach, Florida, have a traditional European Colonial style, which is somehow sweeter."*
>
> —BOBBY McALPINE, ARCHITECT

A Room with a View

ROSEMARY BEACH, FLORIDA

Soaring windows and comfortable,
uncluttered furnishings give
coastal dwellers what they want
most—great gathering spaces and
constant views of the beach.

Of Sandals and Beach Houses

*Built sturdily and for low maintenance, this beachfront
residence at Pensacola has a look appropriate to its setting. It also
draws into itself a full sense of the sea.*

by PHILIP MORRIS

There is an appropriate way to dress for
the beach. There's also an appropriate
way to build. The wrong house on the
beach can look as out of place as saddle
oxfords sunk in sand.

By this analogy, the Lindley Camp
residence at Pensacola Beach is indeed
a sandal.

Designed to be durable, comfortable,
and casually suited to its setting, it's a
good fit. Contemporary, the house still
has much the same feeling as the sketch
of a weathered old coastal dwelling in
the Camps' living room.

The durability of the Camp house, designed by Architect Ellis Bullock, Jr.,
AIA, of Pensacola, is almost a story in
itself. "The beach is about the harshest
environment we have to face in the
South. It should always be taken into
account," observes Bullock. The account
the house takes of its Gulf location is
multiple and thorough.

—The house is raised almost 9 feet
above ground level on piers, protecting
it from possible high water and giving
the living areas better views out to the
bay.

—Concrete block piers are reinforced
with steel rods plus poured concrete and
are tied downward into two concrete
grade beams (laid the length of the
house, below ground level) and upward

to the house itself by means of metal
hurricane clips (anchoring piers to floor
joists).

—Materials: The ⅝-inch red cedar
paneling that encloses the house weath-
ers to a silver gray and turns only love-
lier the more it's exposed. Concrete
block piers are also left natural. Screen-

ing across the ample open-air decks is
noncorroding vinyl.

The comfort given the Camps by the
house relates directly again to how it
makes the most of the beachfront site.
On the street side, where there is really
nothing to see, the house is neutral and
nearly blank (though the facade's sculp-

*Left—On the side facing the street ap-
proach, the Camp house is closed except for
redwood jalousie windows. The ground
level is open except for the stair-entry. The
weathering cedar exterior and reflective
white roof adapt well to the rigorous seacoast location. A three-story stair tower
separates the sleeping side (to the left)
from the living side of house. Right—This
view across the living area and screened-
in deck shows the colorful, light-hearted
furnishings used throughout the house. The
bright-yellow cabinet displays seashells.*
Photographs: Bob Lancaster

CITY HOME

——

A refined uptown house is the epitome of high Southern style.

Southern Classic
MEMPHIS, TENNESSEE

Traditional furnishings, luxe
fabrics, and rich colors come
together for interiors that are at
once genteel and cosmopolitan.

EXPLORING AN ELEGANT, SOPHISTICATED HOME is like meeting an elegant, sophisticated dinner guest. You can count on both for lively conversation, wry wit, and an uncanny knack for making you feel both comfortable and curious. With each new encounter, you will be more intrigued than before. Attribute their appeal to layered experience, an air of unflappable confidence, and a refusal to be swayed or impressed by fleeting trends.

While uptown living in other parts of the country might just as easily take a modern turn, the classic *Southern Living* city home usually begins with traditional architecture and a formal design aesthetic. Modernism, so popular on the West Coast when *Southern Living* launched, has never resonated in the South. While Homes department editors like Louis Joyner and Philip Morris initially set out to find great examples of modern homes, the magazine soon stopped looking for them—and stopped looking west for direction—embracing instead the traditional architecture that spoke to Southern readers.

An elegant city home reflects that traditional Southern style taken to the nth degree. Such a house will be gracious and polished. It will be layered with luxurious textures, bold colors, and tasteful patterns. Fine antiques will pair with comfortable upholstered pieces. Hardwoods might be covered with beautiful old Oriental rugs—or sisal if there are kids in the house.

Contemporary homeowners want comfort, even in an upscale home. Clean-lined chairs might be slipcovered in a fabric that can withstand visits from the four-legged members of the family. A casual outdoor seating area could undercut the formality of a walled garden.

While the major tenets of traditional design have endured, talented designers across the region have added their signature interpretations, keeping classic Southern style fresh and exciting. It's their interesting mix of furnishings and accessories, coupled with the good bones of traditional architecture, that makes these homes special. And it's the fascinating blend of comfort, style, and personality that makes us want to linger there.

Geary Residence

NEW ORLEANS, LOUISIANA

Old Guard decorating tropes
are adapted to modern living
for a relaxed take on New
Orleans formality.

Past Meets Present
The Crescent City inspires a blend of old and new in the Geary House, with upholstered seating surrounding a sleek acrylic table.

Idea House Success

AUGUST 1992

For years, the August issue always seemed to lack the right chemistry to attract readers and advertisers. But then in the early 1990s, Editor in Chief John Floyd decided to make the Idea Houses the star of this issue. The editorial and advertising departments collaborated on a major annual section that gave readers a tour of the Idea Houses and a wealth of inspiration to take away. Problem solved.

Traditional Charm
In the Geary House, one antique piece brings the right touch of Old World elegance to a fresh, modern space.

THE SOUTHERN COLLECTOR

Contrary to popular myth, Southerners do not live in the past. We do, however, relish living with it. We have a penchant for mixing the old and the new, particularly in our homes and gardens. And while we don't hold a monopoly on collecting antiques and vintage pieces, our motivation is uniquely Southern, as Virginia-based antiques dealer Sumpter Priddy told *Southern Living* in a 2014 interview: "In the North, it's all about the academic subtleties. In the South,

it's more about where it came from and who owned it."

A few yards of fine velvet from Great-aunt Effie becomes a dresser scarf. One stairway, stylishly done, can tell the story of many generations as historic pictures, yellowed with age, are framed alongside casual family beach portraits.

Similarly, we collect cuttings from the roses, hydrangeas, and gardenias of our parents and grandparents, bringing these flowers together in the garden just

as we would bring family and friends together around the table. Daffodil bulbs from a country farmhouse are transported to the suburbs, blooming with sunny reminders of home every spring.

There's a poem by Wallace Stevens called "Not Ideas About the Thing But the Thing Itself." Southern collectors would likely reverse that sentiment. It's not just the things themselves we treasure, but the ideas and emotions they conjure.

A Different Drummer Gallery

THOMASVILLE, GEORGIA

Hidden gardens and courtyards, particularly in the city, create a sense of both discovery and escape.

168 Years Old and Still Going Strong

Built about 1810, this Charleston house has had a checkered past. Extensive restoration has brought it back to its original use.

by LOUIS JOYNER

Y ou won't find 20 Burns Lane in any guidebook of Charleston. Originally built as a middle-class residence, it lacked the ornamentation and the refinement of the larger houses below Broad Street. But the house has a certain simple, straight-forward charm, made richer by the rugged brick-work and clean lines; and this extensive restoration preserves that feeling.

According to the owner and restorer, Landscape Architect Robert C. Chesnut, little is known of its past. Rumors say the house was used as a saloon, a bordello, and even as a stable.

What is known for sure is that the house was used as a warehouse for a furniture store since the 1920's. When Chesnut bought the house a few years ago, it had no plumbing or electrical wiring at all.

But the basic brick shell was intact. Although the house had to be completely gutted and rebuilt inside, the basic exterior form was unaltered. The compact, 18- x 39-foot, two-story structure consists of two rooms on each floor as well as two smaller rooms in the attic. The brick walls at the front and rear of the house extend up as parapeted gables. The roof is tin.

As with many houses in Charleston, this house is turned at a right angle to the street. Thus the entrance is located back from the street and at the center of the house. The portion of the side court alongside the house is paved and used for parking. At the rear of the house, the court widens and becomes a brick patio area for outdoor entertaining. A double gate, which is constructed of lattice, separates the parking area

Turned at a right angle to the street, the house creates a side court that is used for parking. This building style, characterized by two rooms to a floor, is referred to as the Charleston Single House. Before restoration, the house was used as a warehouse. Only the brick shell could be salvaged.

A shallow brick arch frames the simple front door. Wood frames for all openings had to be replaced.

from the patio. A stuccoed concrete block wall encloses the patio area on the other two sides.

Inside, on the first floor, the two main rooms are now used as a dining room and as a studio-office. The existing heart-

pine floor has been refinished. The compact L-shaped kitchen at the rear of the house was completely redone and a new breakfast area added. Floor-to-ceiling multi-pane windows wrap two sides of the breakfast area, opening it visually to

A small, 8- x 10-foot breakfast room addition opens onto the patio at the rear of the house. The deck above serves the master bedroom.

Floor-to-ceiling, multi-pane windows give the tiny breakfast room a view out to the patio. Drop lamp is an inexpensive industrial fixture.

A high stuccoed wall encloses two sides of the patio. Two-story house in back, originally the carriage house, is now a separate residence.

Photographs: Louis Joyner

Charleston, South Carolina

JULY 1978

Some Southern cities take uptown—and historic downtown—living to a whole new level. *Southern Living* has followed the rebirth of Charleston from the beginning. "I remember walking around the city with Mayor Riley back in his early days, as he shared his plans for the future," said former Senior Writer Karen Lingo. "Watching that actually happen over the years has been amazing."

GARDEN JOURNAL

—

*Growing the South's favorite
plants helps us connect
with our agrarian roots.*

Barr Property

OAK RIDGE, LOUISIANA

Spider lilies, like many longtime
Southern favorites, are so
enduring that they may well
outlive the gardeners who
planted them.

GREAT GARDENS AND GARDENERS exist all over this country. So what key factors coalesce in our region to produce gardens that feel distinctly Southern? You can boil it down to location, plants, style, and people. For us, the South begins south of the Mason-Dixon Line and extends westward to Oklahoma and Texas. Moving south, we cover gardening all the way to the tip of Brownsville, Texas, and Key West, Florida.

And although technically the southern counties of Ohio, Indiana, and Illinois don't belong to the South, many folks there identify with our Southern gardens and lifestyle, and we welcome them.

That's a lot of territory to put under one umbrella. Southern gardens enjoy long, warm summers and short, mild winters. Lots of different plants grow there. Because of the strategic location of many old Southern ports such as Baltimore, Charleston, and New Orleans, exotic plants, including azaleas and camellias, that soon would be considered classics were imported here during colonial times. Historic estates such as Monticello in Virginia and Middleton Place in South Carolina were among the first to display them, and by doing so popularized them across the region.

Of course, not every import liked it here. Iconic plants of New England and northern Europe, such as the common lilac, delphinium, and English

holly, stewed in our Southern latitudes. However, those that survived often had a bigger impact on our Southern gardens than many of our native plants.

Southerners share recipes, stories, dialects, and a regional identity like no other group. We also like to share plants. Many people divide and share plants that are cherished for quirky or valuable traits that make them conversation pieces. We call these heirloom plants "passalongs." Passed down from mother to daughter and friend to friend, many are hard to find in nurseries today and survive mainly in the gardens of the people who used to share them. These plants link us with our past and the people who have gone before. The best part of receiving a passalong plant is that every time you see it in your garden, you instantly remember when you got it and the person who gave it to you.

**Virginia Beach,
Virginia**

MARCH 1972

Sweeping beds of azaleas
surround the terrace, acting
as an informal visual link
between its regular lines and
the existing trees and ground
contours of the site.

Ladew Topiary Gardens

MONKTON, MARYLAND

Public gardens showcasing good
design offer an important teaching
ground for homeowner-gardeners.

Hydrangea Garden

MACON, GEORGIA

According to folklore, a rusty
nail buried near the roots of
mopheads and lacecaps
will change the bloom color
(which is actually dictated by
the soil's pH).

Jenks Farmer, Plantsman
BEECH ISLAND, SOUTH CAROLINA

Southern nurserymen, like Jenks Farmer, have created thriving enterprises while preserving favorite plants and bulbs grown here for generations.

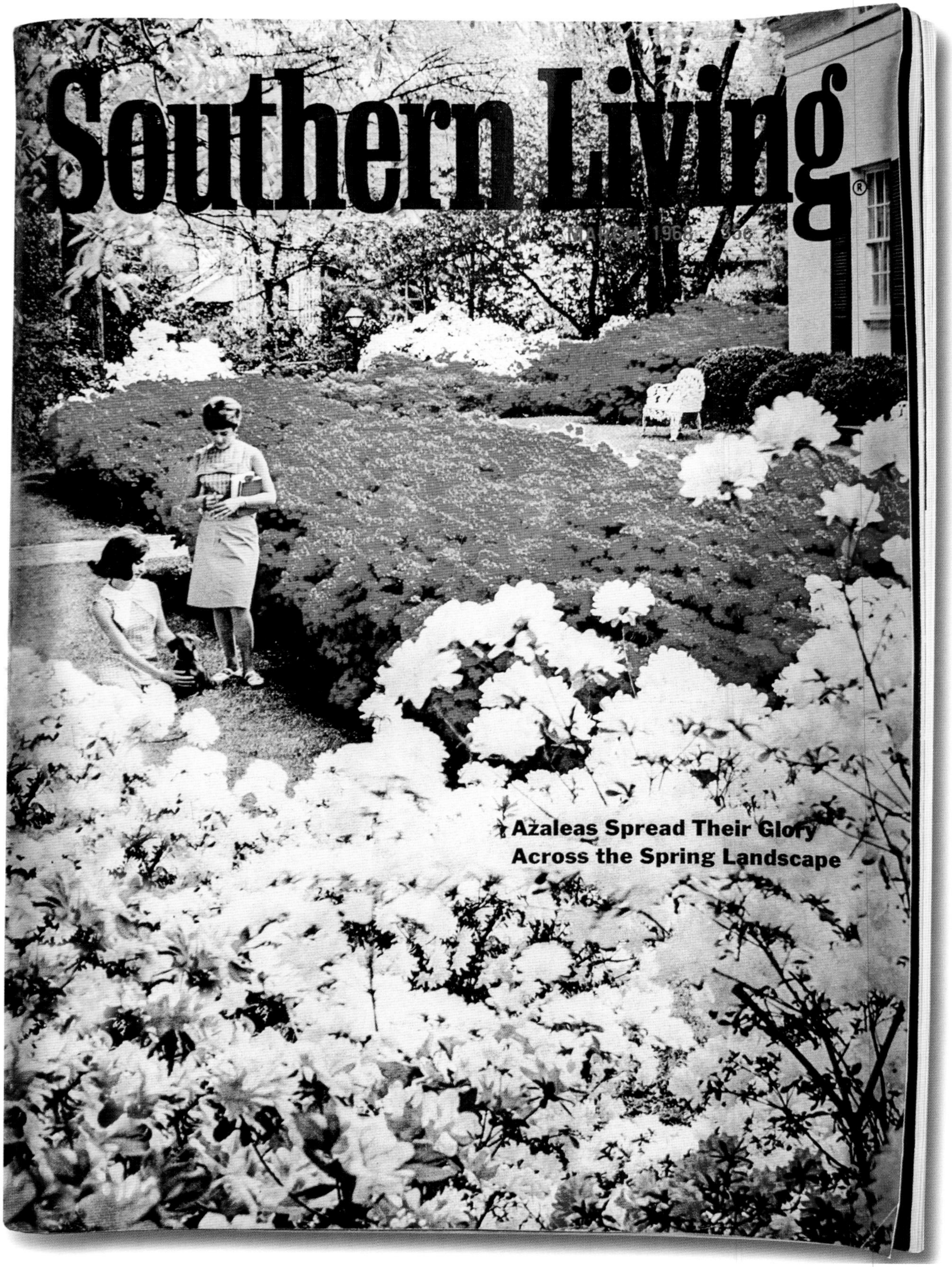
Southern Living
Azaleas Spread Their Glory
Across the Spring Landscape

A LOOK BACK

Symbol of Spring

MARCH 1968

"Every Southern garden should have azaleas," this feature declared. The wildly popular shrub was featured on the very first *Southern Living* cover in February 1966 and made return engagements on many covers that would follow, usually in March or April.

From Our Readers: Great Weekend Escapes

Southern Living

MARCH 1992 • $2.95

Shrubs That Grandma Loved

A Simple Menu That's Springtime Fresh

Home Recycling Can Work for You

GARDEN BONUS

Fix Up the Front Yard

A LOOK BACK

Best Seller

MARCH 1992

This spring cover, featuring a mother and child flanked by hydrangeas, introduced *Southern Living* editors to the power of iconic flowers. Photographed by Van Chaplin in Atlanta, it remains one of the best-selling *Southern Living* issues of all time.

Canyon Kitchen

LONESOME VALLEY,
NORTH CAROLINA

Farm-to-table foods have gotten a boost from Southern chefs, many of whom not only buy fresh ingredients locally but grow their own.

HEIRLOOMS FROM THE VINE

Tomato season is as important to the South as football season, which is saying a lot. We love it because it is fleeting and must be enjoyed in the moment. We love it because it is unchanging, a reliable pleasure we can anticipate year after year. No hot-house tomato purchased from the supermarket will ever taste the same as a fresh heirloom plucked from the vine on a hot summer afternoon.

There are two kinds of gardeners in the South—those who have grown tomatoes and those who will grow them.

No other crop produces so much for so many for so little expense. Just about everyone swears by his or her own favorite method of growing tomatoes. If yours works, you better stick with it.

According to Texas songwriting legend Guy Clark, there are "only two things that money can't buy, that's true love and homegrown tomatoes"—a fact that leaves us longing all winter long for the perfect summer sandwich. It's incredibly hard to beat the iconic

soft-white-bread Southern classic, especially when there's homemade mayo involved and the tomatoes are still warm from the backyard sun. Learning to grow tomatoes is a rite of passage for Southerners, something we believe we should know how to do—like making a decent pan of cornbread, setting a proper table, or baking the perfect pound cake. And it's especially satisfying to grow an heirloom, a deliciously singular garden treasure. Building the perfect tomato sandwich is an art form.

The New Southern Farm

BY STEVE BENDER

SOUTHERN LIVING SENIOR EDITOR

I GREW UP EATING THE BEST FOOD IN THE WORLD. It wasn't boxed, canned, emulsified, stabilized, enriched, artificially colored, flash-frozen, irradiated, government-inspected, bought, or sold. It was fresh vegetables and fruit born from the earth that was nurtured, tilled, and toiled over by my mother's family in the Sandhills of North Carolina. That bounty was an epiphany to a Maryland boy like me, inured to slurping down cling peaches in heavy syrup.

Every August through the 1960s, my parents and brothers and I would make the arduous 8-hour drive from Baltimore to the Sandhills in our un-air-conditioned Rambler station wagon—essentially, a gray Dutch oven on wheels. Our payoff was eating classic, home-style Southern food at a different relative's house each night.

Biblical amounts of homegrown veggies were served. Second and third helpings were law. Into the bottomless pit of my adolescent stomach fell green beans, butter beans, Southern peas, coleslaw, collards, ears of 'Silver Queen' corn when they were sweet, and scoops of stewed corn when they got starchy. Sliced tomatoes were omnipresent, of course—a mixed blessing since I didn't like raw tomatoes, which was considered sinful.

Okra stood tall on the highest rung of my gastronomical ladder. If you grew okra in Baltimore, people regarded you with suspicion, like you might be a closet Republican or victim of alien visitation. But okra in the Sandhills was de rigueur. Folks there prepared it the only way it should ever be eaten—battered in cornmeal, sprinkled with salt and pepper, and deep-fried in lard. When Grandma was making it, I'd sit in the kitchen and stare at the simmering skillet, mesmerized. "A watched pot never boils," she'd say to curb my ravenous impatience. Even though her metaphor didn't apply to frying at all, I thought this sounded wise and still do.

All of my mother's kin had gardens, mostly from necessity. If you wanted vegetables in winter, you grew and canned them. They kept animals too—chickens for eggs and meat and cows for milk. My mother recalls coming home from school one day and discovering to her horror that someone had tied the family cow out front by the street. Everyone knew that respectable folks kept their cows in back.

By the mid-sixties, however, seeds of change had already been sown both for backyard gardeners and the small family farm. Small farms got gobbled up by big farms that instead of growing a little of lots of things grew lots of

226

one thing. And as the middle class fled the cities, new housing developments sliced up sold-off pasturelands like pecan pies at Thanksgiving.

By the time *The Progressive Farmer* launched *Southern Living* in 1966, the number of U.S. farms had dropped from more than six million during the Depression to around two million. Readers shifted their focus from tractors and hog futures to decorating, landscaping, and entertaining in the new suburbs. *Southern Living* wisely covered those topics for a newly growing and prosperous South. Its circulation soared, making it the biggest regional lifestyle magazine in the country, a rank it still holds.

Turning farms into lawns, pools, and beds of azaleas came with a price. For the first time, a generation of Southerners lost touch with its agrarian roots. No longer did you have to grow things as a hedge against winter or a bad year. You could buy mass-produced vegetables and fruits sealed in cans and jars that would last about forever. Fresh milk and eggs stopped being delivered to your door from local farms. Instead, you bought them from a supermarket chain. Foods that shipped well from hundreds of miles away supplanted less rugged local delicacies and heirloom varieties handed down from family member to family member. Taste and quirkiness lost out to uniformity and price. Southerners wound up consuming the same things everybody else did.

But you can eat bad food for only so long, unless you're English. As Southerners traveled and tried new foods, they discovered that cardboard is not a flavor, ripe beats unripe, fresh trumps artificially preserved, taste wins out over convenience, and eating locally grown specialties is much more interesting. Why limit yourself to a ubiquitous 'Red Delicious' apple shipped cross-country from Washington State when you can experience the spicy-sweet flesh of an heirloom 'Grimes Golden' apple that was discovered in West Virginia in 1804?

"Eat local" is a Southern mantra today. It manifests itself all across the food spectrum. Fine restaurants often source their vegetables, fruits, cheeses, wines, and meats from nearby family farms that emphasize freshness, variety, and sustainable farming methods. These establishments proudly identify the sources on the menu.

Community supported agriculture is another welcome development. Participating CSA farmers sell memberships that allow consumers to buy fresh, seasonal produce directly from them. The earnings generated enrich local economies while the fresh vegetables and fruits consumed enrich our diets.

The most visible evidence of the "eat fresh, eat local" revolution is the rise of farmers' markets. These markets don't limit themselves to selling vegetables and fruits. Stroll through them and you'll find locally produced eggs, honey, bread, cakes, pies, herbs, sausages, jellies, cheeses, syrups, cider, flowers, and more.

And it's the South where the numbers of farmers' markets are growing the fastest. According to the USDA's 2014 National Farmers Market Directory, five of the 10 states with the biggest increases are Southern —Tennessee, Louisiana, Texas, Arkansas, and North Carolina. A big reason for that is the yearning for traditional Southern staples and regional varieties that our grandparents grew and we grew up on. There's no taste like home.

"Turning farms into lawns, pools, and beds of azaleas came with a price."

3
SOUTHERN TABLE

So many great dishes have made

their way across the South because of one simple question: Could I get that recipe? ◆ In its very first issue, *Southern Living* began asking readers to share their favorite dishes, but initially only about 25 percent of its recipes came from those home cooks. ◆ Like most magazines and newspapers at the time, *Southern Living* got the bulk of its recipes, along with accompanying black-and-white images, from national food companies such as Pillsbury and Betty Crocker. ◆ Generally, these recipes were not retested. The idea of building a food section around reader recipes would later set

Southern Living

JULY 1977 · $1.00

Breezy, Easy
Tablecloths
From Sheets

A Celebration
Of Air and Space

Build Your Own Lattice

Drama in the
Out of Doors

Summer Suppers
A Special Section

A LOOK BACK

Summer Suppers

JULY 1977

No one knows how to throw a party quite like a Southerner. And whether it's Holiday Dinners, Reunions, or Summer Suppers, special sections on food and entertaining have always been popular with our readers.

the magazine apart from its competitors but also would require the editors to rethink their kitchen space. The original galley-style Test Kitchen was so ill-equipped that founding Food Editor Lena Sturges would frequently bypass it altogether and take her assistants to her home to prepare recipes.

One of the young home economists chopping, baking, and stirring in that kitchen was Jean Wickstrom Liles, who succeeded her friend and mentor after Sturges became gravely ill and had to leave. Once Liles became Food Editor in 1976, she and *Southern Living* Editor Gary McCalla committed to making reader recipes a hallmark of the magazine, calling for them more and more frequently.

As the magazine grew in popularity, the trickle of submissions quickly swelled to a deluge, with thousands of handwritten recipes arriving every month. Along with the recipes came letters and postcards, which played a vital role in educating the staff about how Southerners were eating, cooking, and entertaining; where they were grocery shopping; how much they were spending; and most of all, what they wanted from the magazine. "Reader involvement," Liles said, "was part of the magic of *Southern Living*."

Liles was building on the audience engagement Sturges had begun. In 1973, *Southern Living* had moved into a modern headquarters with a kitchen that was much improved over the old one but would soon become inadequate to handle the volume of recipes that needed to be tested. Two additional kitchens were added in 1978, and when the magazine moved to an even larger headquarters in 1989, *Southern Living* would expand to eight Test Kitchens, all designed to mimic the home cook's experience and help guarantee that the magazine's recipes were absolutely fail-safe.

The popularity and reliability of *Southern Living* recipes, coupled with a steady flow of comments, questions, and suggestions from readers, led to highly successful extensions of the brand. A best-selling book series, *Southern Living Annual Recipes*, was launched in 1979. Subscribers often wrote to say that they clipped recipes from the magazine—and didn't like doing it one bit. The solution was *Annual Recipes*, which has sold over 21 million copies since its first printing.

Another by-product of reader mail was the "Cooking Light" column. Since the late seventies, readers had been writing to ask for help in reducing salt, sugar, and fat in their diets and generally eating healthier. In 1982, McCalla agreed to add a new column dedicated to healthy cooking and to hire a registered dietitian. Readers and advertisers loved the new editorial, and their enthusiasm paved the

way for *Cooking Light* magazine a few years later. (The first issue, a newsstand edition, was produced by the *Southern Living* staff, just as *The Progressive Farmer* had helped launch *Southern Living*.)

But the most popular recipes in *Southern Living* weren't the healthiest. They were the cakes, pies, and decadent treats—the showstoppers—and the magazine made stars out of the readers who created them. It published contributors' names and hometowns, along with their recipes. Besides a couple of nominal gifts, it sent each of them a set of *Southern Living* recipe cards printed with their published dishes. Contributors would proudly give these to friends and family, promoting the magazine as they passed along their recipes. As part of the Silver Jubilee in 1990, *Southern Living* invited 12 of its best recipe contributors over the years—"Cooks Across the South"—to come to Birmingham, test recipes with the staff, be featured in the magazine, and enjoy the royal treatment, Southern style.

Over time, readers developed such a strong bond with *Southern Living* Foods that they were willing to follow the editors into uncharted territory. In 1986, Deborah Garrison Lowery interviewed four young Dallas chefs and introduced readers to the brand-new food they were creating—the now ubiquitous Southwest cuisine.

Since then, modern media and technology have exponentially broadened the culinary horizons of Southern cooks. With the click of a mouse or the TV remote, readers easily can be exposed to cooking traditions from around the world. But they continue coming to *Southern Living* for an informed interpretation of the South's unique food story.

And our story grows more interesting each year as talented chefs inspire us, not only by elevating classic regional foods but also by blending those dishes with cooking traditions from their own heritage. You might find, on the menu, Maw Maw's Ravioli at Andrew Michael Italian Kitchen in Memphis, dumplings served with Korean Braised Goat at Underbelly in Houston, and Stone Ground Baked Grits with country ham, mushrooms, and fresh thyme at Highlands Bar and Grill in Birmingham.

Whether taking readers on a culinary adventure or teaching them the best techniques for tried-and-true favorites, *Southern Living* has always known that its recipes are about so much more than getting supper on the table. "The food that we presented was like an offering to the reader," said former Senior Food Editor Mary Allen Perry. "It would be something they would share when they entertained or just cooked for their loved ones. We knew they were depending on those recipes to work."

Jane Elliot and Margaret Chason Agnew

Karen Parker

Former Editor Gary McCalla joins taste-testing

Peggy Smith and Jane Cairns

Kaye Adams and Patty Vann

Robbie Melvin, Angela Sellers, Norman King, Whitney Wright, and Pam Lolley

TESTING 1-2-3

Systems are everything, especially when nearly 5,000 recipes are pouring in each month. In the mid-seventies, *Southern Living* began developing an elaborate system of filing, testing, rating, and editing recipes that not only went a long way toward ensuring success for the home cook but also gave the Food staff additional tools for answering reader calls and letters. Once the editors combined foolproof recipes with a communication style that was personal and approachable, they had hit upon the essence of their brand: a powerful bond with a fiercely loyal audience.

It began, as so many things do in the South, around the table, where *Southern Living* established a rigorous system of testing. Not only would recipes be evaluated for taste, appearance, cost, availability of ingredients, and ease of preparation, but the staff would learn to anticipate difficulties or variables that could trip up the home cook. Grilled foods might be tested on both gas and charcoal. The same batter or filling might be beaten with both a stand mixer and a hand mixer to determine whether texture and consistency were affected. Groceries would be purchased locally, rather than ordered commercially, to make sure ingredients would be available at a typical suburban supermarket.

The Food staff would gather daily in the Test Kitchen for taste-testing, evaluating more than 100 recipes each week and taking careful editing notes to ensure clarity for the reader. Some dishes failed with no hope of redemption; some passed but were retested to make them even better; and others passed with no retesting required. Those that passed were immediately rated by the staff. Initially, *Southern Living* used a basic 1 to 3 scale: 1=good, 2=very good, 3=perfect. Later, they recognized subtle nuances in quality by adding pluses: 1, 1+, 2, 2+, 3.

"The rating system was really designed to help the staff answer reader requests," explained former Food Editor Jean Wickstrom Liles. "Sometimes we would be taste-testing and a reader would call in and ask for 'the best chocolate cake *Southern Living* has ever published.' An Editorial Assistant who went to the files would have no way of knowing which one that was. I decided we really needed to rate the recipes while we were taste-testing so that anybody on the staff could take that reader call, go to the files, and easily find the best ones."

After taste-testing, the staff would package any leftovers and take them home to their families to see how "real people" responded. "We were working

moms, and if we had leftovers we would not throw them away," remembers Peggy Smith, who was the first member of the original *Southern Living* Test Kitchen staff. "My kids and their best friends still talk about those packets in my refrigerator. They got to try things that probably no other kids got to try."

Marian Cooper Cairns remembers those leftovers. When she joined the Test Kitchen staff, she was following in the footsteps of her mother, Jane, who would bring home Test Kitchen fare on Chinet plates in zip-top bags. Cairns recalled her job interview in the May 2010 issue of the magazine: "Here I was at the same dining table where my mother had taste-tested recipes for so many years, with editors who had known her. One of them said, 'Marian's a legacy,' just as if I were joining a sorority."

That familial atmosphere has informed the way the staff approaches food—as something to share and pass down, something wonderful that you can always count on. "My son's whole wedding reception was done by *Southern Living* staff," Smith remembers. "Each of the Test Kitchen staff contributed a dish. [Former Senior Food Photographer] Charles Walton did the photography. We all keep in touch. My years there aren't so much about work as family."

Test Kitchen

1977

Former Food Editor Jean Wickstrom Liles and the *Southern Living* Test Kitchen staff re-created the home cook experience. They wanted to be sure that the recipes contained ingredients that were widely available at local grocery stores.

SIGNATURE SOUTHERN

—

These are the storied dishes that have graced our tables for generations and become synonymous with the South.

FRIED CHICKEN, BISCUITS, GUMBO, POTATO SALAD—these are the classic Southern dishes we hand down from one generation to the next. Over time, we memorize the ingredients from recipe cards handwritten by our mothers, mastering technique by watching great family cooks show us how it's done. And although we might occasionally try a new twist on an old favorite, we always seem to return to the version we grew up with.

Maybe that's because all signature Southern dishes are equal parts flavor and emotion, connecting us with people and places we love. Stir together a bowl of potato salad and you will no doubt hear your mother's voice reminding you that it *must* be made with Hellmann's (unless, of course, she says it *must* be made with Duke's). Bake your great-aunt's "famous" pound cake and you'll immediately conjure memories of the family reunions and church socials where you first enjoyed it.

"Pound cakes, like potato salad, are such a personal thing—more so, really, than other cakes," said former Senior Food Editor Mary Allen Perry, who developed scores of cakes for

Southern Living, including the annual December cover cake. "So many families have their own particular recipe. When I asked readers to send their favorites in 1976, I got almost 300 handwritten stories about what that particular cake meant to that individual family. They were really beautiful and very touching."

That's what's so special about these Southern dishes—they tell our story. They help us define who we are and where we came from. That gives them the power to transport. Even if we were a thousand miles from the nearest pitcher of sweet tea, one taste of the country ham or fried chicken we grew up with would carry us, through memory, back to the South.

"Ham held the same rating as the little black dress. If you had a ham in the meat house, any situation could be faced."

EDNA LEWIS, *THE TASTE OF COUNTRY COOKING*, 1976

Brown Sugar-Bourbon-Glazed Ham, page 294

Chicken-and-Sausage
Gumbo, page 296

240

Our Best Southern Fried Chicken, page 294

Perfect Pot of Grits,
page 296

Our Favorite Buttermilk
Biscuit, page 297

The Ultimate Classic
Collards, page 295

Grannie's Cracklin
Cornbread, page 296

Southern Living

JULY 1968 • 35¢

World's Largest
Watermelon Cutting

Watermelon Cutting

JULY 1968

Many of the early issues of the magazine covered nostalgic Southern events such as Watermelon Day in Atlanta, Georgia. Over 30,000 watermelon-loving Georgians gathered to celebrate this summertime favorite and see the crowning of the melon-eating champion.

243

Basic White Cake with
Peppermint Frosting, page 297

THE CAKES OF *SOUTHERN LIVING*

Call us shameless name-droppers, but Southerners have a habit of honoring places and people, real or fictional, by naming cakes after them.

In the late 1800s, Emma Rylander Lane, of Clayton, Alabama, took first prize at the county fair with her sponge cake iced with a fluffy white frosting. She originally called the recipe Prize Cake, but friends convinced her to make the cake her namesake, and today you'll likely find Lane Cake served at a family's noteworthy occasions. *Southern Living* first published a recipe for Lane Cake in the second issue in 1966.

Along with Mrs. Lane, other cakes honoring people and places include Lord and Lady Baltimore Cake and Martha Washington's Great Cake. Other Southern-bred cakes include rich caramel cake, red velvet cake, and the *Southern Living* favorite, Hummingbird Cake (pictured above in our February 1978 issue), submitted by Mrs. L.H. Wiggins.

While a few of these cakes may rarely appear on today's tables, the art of cake baking remains a point of great pride among Southern cooks, and now, as in colonial days, the type of cake served still conveys, to a degree, the status of the occasion. Cakes made with available ingredients like everyday pound cakes and upside-down skillet cakes are for family; those made with previously hard-to-get ingredients like citrus fruit or coconut are reserved for weddings and holidays.

And perhaps there's no cake in the South quite as important as the cake served on the holiday table. In 1995, *Southern Living* put a photograph of a three-layer Coconut-Lemon Cake on the cover. The overwhelming reader response to this cake began a tradition of "the big white cake," as the staff knows it, adorning the cover every December.

Key Lime Pound Cake,
page 298

Southern Living

THANKSGIVING CELEBRATIONS

93 Holiday Recipes!
Southern-Style Turkeys
Showstopping Desserts
Sensational Sides

Brown Sugar
Bourbon Bundt
PAGE 117

Black Bottom
Pumpkin Pie
PAGE 116

OUR 10 BEST CAKES & PIES

PLUS

NOVEMBER 2012

$4.99US $6.50CAN

STYLISH WAYS
TO SET
YOUR TABLE

50 REASONS WE'RE
THANKFUL
TO BE SOUTHERN

Holiday Desserts

NOVEMBER 2012

The reputation of many Southern cooks is tied to a great dessert. So each year we make sure that our holiday special issues are jam-packed with dozens of showstopping sweets that are sure to be the talk of any holiday table.

THE *SOUTHERN LIVING* COOKING SCHOOL

Before the Food Network or the Cooking Channel, before chefs such as Bobby Flay and Ina Garten were household names, the *Southern Living* Cooking School was crisscrossing the South, sharing its food know-how with an eager audience. From 1978 through 2000, it presented live cooking demonstrations to more than 120,000 eager *Southern Living* fans annually.

"It was initially set up as a way to lock in advertising," explained Martha Johnston, who was recruited to lead the Cooking School. "Advertisers paid a fee to have their products promoted and demonstrated onstage, and they committed to a certain number of ad pages."

Cooking Schools were presented in large auditoriums by five show teams. Each two-member team included a food and entertaining specialist, who did the cooking demonstrations, and a program coordinator, who worked with local media, coordinated setup, and emceed the shows. In fact, the Cooking School staff at one time was larger than the *Southern Living* Test Kitchen staff.

This onstage team was just part of the puzzle, however. A local newspaper or radio/TV station would co-sponsor the show and arrange for a charity in town to provide volunteer assistants. Part of the proceeds would help support that charity. A retail grocer would supply ingredients for the show. Meanwhile, the Cooking School would alert key buyers at grocery stores across the South to let them know what products they were promoting and what food features were coming up in the magazine.

Many of the national food companies who sponsored the Cooking School did so because they weren't reaching the South. The Cooking School would develop great recipes that Southerners loved, incorporating the advertisers' products. In the eighties, one advertiser saw the market share for a new piecrust jump to 65 percent in the South, all because the Cooking School taught consumers how to use it and where to find it in the grocery store.

Over time, changes in demographics and technology reshaped the Cooking School. Daytime shows were eliminated as more women joined the workforce. Video replaced slide photography onstage, and then the live show was eliminated altogether in 2001, when the magazine shifted to a program of in-store cooking videos. Even so, readers fondly remember the traveling show, and Johnston still gets a familiar question: "When are y'all coming back?"

Taking the Stage
BIRMINGHAM, ALABAMA

The Cooking School published collections of recipes each year and would demonstrate selected dishes at events around the South to packed audiences.

FARM TO TABLE

—

Southerners have long understood the connection between good earth and good food.

Hampstead Farms

MONTGOMERY, ALABAMA

This community in
the heart of the Deep South
hosts farm-to-table dinners.

WHEN *SOUTHERN LIVING* CAME ALONG, the region was still no more than a generation removed from the farm. Later, as the gap between suburbs and the farmstead widened, such culinary traditions as canning, pickling, and preserving fell out of favor. Now they're back but reinterpreted for the modern South, where

backyard gardens and patio containers have replaced the acres of fruits and vegetables our parents and grandparents grew.

As *Southern Living* assembled its first editorial team and proclaimed itself "The Magazine of the Modern South," its rural roots were evident, despite its urban vision. Before joining *The Progressive Farmer*, Food Editor Lena Sturges had traveled for the Extension Service, working with rural communities across her native Texas. By the time *Southern Living* was launched, not only had Sturges produced magazine articles that helped Southern cooks improve their skills in the kitchen, but she had likely given them hands-on instruction in those kitchens over the years.

For decades, *Southern Living* maintained a tradition of teaching and inspiring cooks to enjoy the fresh bounty of the South. Today, many Southern families are growing their own food again, not out of necessity but out of a desire to reconnect with something healthy and genuine.

Canning and pickling have made a comeback, but instead of going to a community hall for instruction by a county agent, modern cooks surf the Internet, amass cookbooks, and watch food television to gather ideas and advice. All three of those powerful media outlets have helped fuel a revival of farm-to-table cooking by providing a huge platform for celebrity chefs, many of whom are vocal proponents of fresh, locally sourced ingredients. In a 2014 interview with *Southern Living*, Canadian-born chef Hugh Acheson, now chef-partner at several notable Georgia restaurants, described canning as "a rekindling of a relationship with your immediate community, which is your family, and a bigger community, your farmers' market and the hardware store where you buy your jars."

Whether they're growing heirloom tomatoes, building a backyard chicken coop, or just shopping for produce at the local farmers' market, Southern cooks are reaching into the soil and taking hold of their deep-down roots. They are daily making that farm-to-table connection, described by chef Scott Peacock in a 1996 *Southern Living* feature: "The truest Southern food is immediate. It's harvested, fussed over, then eaten that day."

Heirloom Tomato
Salad, page 300

This farm-to-table menu includes, clockwise from top left: Minty Lemonade (page 301); Spinach-and-Three-Herb Pesto (page 303) on eggs; Kale-and-Blueberry Slaw with Buttermilk Dressing (page 303); Cucumbers with Ginger, Rice Vinegar, and Mint (page 303); and Creamy Basil-Black Pepper Cucumbers (page 303).

"*My favorite Southern dish is okra soup. I like it in the Charleston style with tomatoes and onion. The best is from the Piggly Wiggly just down the road from my house.*"

—DARIUS RUCKER, SINGER, *SOUTHERN LIVING*, DECEMBER 2012

Roasted Sweet Potato-and-Onion Tart, page 300

Tennessee Whiskey-
Pecan Pie, page 301

Southern Living

JUNE 1982 • $2.25

Shopping the South's
Farmers' Markets

Fresh Okra, Fried
And Otherwise

Seaside House Lives
Like an Inn

Caladiums Cool
The Summer

A LOOK BACK

Farmers' Markets

JUNE 1982

In the early days of the rural South, farmers who grew more than their families could consume drove around the neighborhood selling produce from the backs of their wagons. Farmers' markets have grown more popular than ever, and this particular issue shared some of the best found around the South.

PUTTING UP

BY VIRGINIA WILLIS

Like many Southerners, I grew up with canning and preserving. My family always planted a large kitchen garden near the house and often another plot for corn in the fertile soil down by the river. We ate food fresh in season and preserved the garden's goodness for later too. My mother and grandmother taught me to freeze black-eyed peas, butterbeans, and creamed corn; to transform peaches, wild blackberries, and scuppernong grapes into jams and jellies; to can green beans and tomatoes in summer; and to put up peanuts, pears, and spicy chowchow in the fall.

I treasure those memories and our family tradition. While there's something seemingly old-fashioned about what we Southerners call "putting up," preserving remains an integral part of any good Southern cook's repertoire. My family would preserve gallons at a time in all-day marathons, both at home and at community canning centers.

No matter the size of the batch, there's something amazingly satisfying about preserving food. I love the aroma of vinegar and warm spices and the impromptu steam facial I get while making pickles. I smile every time I hear the subtle pop of a lid dimpling down on a cooling jar, the telltale sign of a successful seal. To see colorful jars cooling on a windowsill—with the sun illuminating them like stained glass—is delicious in more ways than one.

Southern Living

AUGUST 1981 · $1.95

Pickle Your Own Crops

Periwinkle Takes the Heat

A House on the Rocks

**Special Feature:
The New
River**

Pickle Your Crops

AUGUST 1981

Southern Living has always led the way on Southern food trends. This feature revived the almost-forgotten art of canning not just for economy, but also for the wonderful homemade flavors and the satisfaction that comes from preserving the summer garden to enjoy all year.

Rise of the Southern Chef

BY JOHN CURRENCE

CHEF OF CITY GROCERY IN OXFORD, MISSISSIPPI, AND OTHER RESTAURANTS AROUND THE SOUTH

I N A CORNER OF THE COUNTRY where the largest canon of regional food was built on the backs of home cooks, pioneers, struggling immigrants, slaves, servants, and farmers, it is interesting and ironic to consider the chef's role in the ascension of Southern cuisine. Chefs have become celebrities, restaurateurs are modern day P.T. Barnums, dining room decor is high art, and dinner service is theater. Over the last 30 years, we've seen a dramatic shift in the racial and gender makeup of the Southern kitchen. Today ours is a club filled largely with doughy, waspy, white men—not exactly a group that represents the originators of our tradition.

It is a black, self-proclaimed socialist from middle Virginia we should credit for sparking the interest in Southern food. Edna Lewis' fortuitous landing at Café Nicholson on New York's Upper East Side in 1949 shined a credible light on the foodways of the South. Miss Lewis, who had come to the city with little in the way of career ambition, worked briefly at a dry cleaners and sewed in one of the more prestigious fashion houses before she fell into cooking. Under her direction, Café Nicholson quickly attracted Southern expats who were hungry for the food of their home tables. Word spread. William Faulkner, Tennessee Williams, Richard Avedon, Marlene Dietrich, and Marlon Brando, among others, became regulars. She began jotting down notes about her food, which became *The Edna Lewis Cookbook*, published in 1972. This was the first of her many books that have influenced the definition of modern Southern cooking.

If the fire was lit in the forties, then it really caught in the early eighties. Within months of each other in 1982, Frank Stitt and Bill Neal opened, respectively, Highlands Bar and Grill in Birmingham, Alabama, and Crook's Corner in Chapel Hill, North Carolina. Frank and Bill, both classically trained, opened these venues with the intention of exploring the food from their families' tables. Frank, raised just north of Birmingham, would examine Southern cuisine more identified with the African-American tradition and refine those dishes with precise European technique. Bill, from the Lowcountry of South Carolina, picked apart his mother's and grandmother's food—everything from shrimp and grits to Huguenot torte—and brought them together for the first time at a fine dining restaurant.

Bill's kitchen was a dizzying place to work for me as a young cook. He darted on and off the line. New ideas for dishes swirled around the place. New purveyors constantly offered their services, and people fought for positions behind the stove. The little hotbox of a kitchen was alive with energy and excitement, and Bill's enthusiasm was infectious. What was happening at Crook's was the beginning of a "thing." None of us understood entirely what the "thing" was, but we knew we were in the thick of it and just needed to hang on for the ride.

The real catalyst for national interest in Southern food was a visit from Craig Claiborne to the Chapel Hill area in 1985. Claiborne, a native Mississippian, had helmed the food section of *The New York Times* for a decade. Though very much a fixture in New York, he was nostalgic for the food, humor, and culture of the South.

He wrote an astonishing feature in the *Times*, on June 26, 1985, trumpeting the food of the new South and the young chefs who were leading the charge. Claiborne waxed poetic about everything from the she-crab soup at Crook's Corner to the fried chicken at Mama Dip's Country Kitchen. He followed up with a second feature on Bill Neal in July of that same summer. Claiborne's benediction touched on Bill's grasp of the nuances of Southern food and his deep understanding of its historical roots. Claiborne wrote, "[Neal] considers the regional dishes of this country as important and worthy of preservation as the nation's monuments and architecture." It was an anointing moment for Southern food.

Bill's entire philosophy for Crook's Corner rested on the idea that chefs need to celebrate, preserve, and protect the food that came from generations of home cooks, from grandmothers and housekeepers. Our food is meaningful. Our food paints a picture of who we are.

In this moment, chefs across the region were waking to the same realization—Ben and Karen Barker in Durham, Stephan Pyles and Dean Fearing in Dallas, Norman Van Aken in south Florida, Frank Brigtsen and Susan Spicer in New Orleans. Each of them, in their own way, rejected the gross misconception that Southern food was just one big fried thing.

Their work legitimized our cuisine and gave the next generation of chefs, myself included, the freedom to take traditional Southern dishes and apply foreign ingredients or techniques—for instance Szechuan pepper-spiked collards—and also to take Southern ingredients and techniques and apply those to foreign dishes, such as red bean cassoulet.

My peers—with the likes of Ashley Christensen, Anne Quatrano, Edward Lee, John Besh, Linton Hopkins, Tandy Wilson, John Fleer, Chris Hastings, and Donald Link, among many others—started out with the European classics of our training, but we found our voices in the food of our home tables and our childhood. Now the torch is being passed to a group of young men and women who have never known a time when our food lacked respect or dignity. As a result, a legion of chefs are diving straight into their families' recipe cards. Andy Ticer and Michael Hudman of Memphis riff on the traditional Italian foods of their grandmothers' tables. Vivian Howard elevates East Carolina favorites that might otherwise be forgotten and disappear.

The rise of the Southern chef is about the men and women who have chosen to celebrate, document, elevate, and safeguard the flavors that make us such a unique part of the world. It's also about our roots—may we never forget them.

"[Neal] considers the regional dishes of this country as important and worthy of preservation as the nation's monuments."

SOUTHERN CHEFS

It's impossible to name all the chefs who have helped define and promote Southern cuisine over the last five decades, but here are some of the people who have made a profound difference.

Anne Quatrano, Atlanta, Georgia

Chris Shepherd, Houston, Texas

Edna Lewis, Decatur, Georgia

Edward Lee, Louisville, Kentucky

Frank Stitt, Birmingham, Alabama

John Currence, Oxford, Mississippi

Leah Chase, New Orleans, Louisiana

Paul Prudhomme, New Orleans, Louisiana

Sean Brock, Charleston, South Carolina, and Nashville, Tennessee

Ashley Christensen, Raleigh, North Carolina

Bill Smith, Chapel Hill, North Carolina

Vivian Howard, Kinston, North Carolina

Emeril Lagasse, New Orleans, Louisiana

Frank Lee, Charleston, South Carolina

John Besh, New Orleans, Louisiana

Stephan Pyles, Dallas, Texas

Chris Hastings, Birmingham, Alabama

Scott Peacock, Atlanta, Georgia

COMMUNAL TABLE

—

Swapping recipes is just a means to an end—sharing wonderful food together.

Summerland
CARTERSVILLE, GEORGIA

Southern Living brings readers together to share food and memories around the Southern table.

TURN OVER A SOUTHERN COOK'S empty casserole dishes and you will invariably see her name on the bottom, written in nail polish or on a piece of masking tape. Whether the occasion is mournful or celebratory, we believe in "carrying food" to mark it. And whenever we taste an especially fine dish at a neighborhood cookout or family reunion, we've just got to have that recipe.

With its focus on reader recipes, *Southern Living* food became, essentially, a region-wide community cookbook. Some of the recipes we've shared exceeded even the editors' expectations. The Milky Way Cake that appeared on the cover in August 1977 all but sold out its namesake candy bar across the South. It doesn't grace many fellowship halls these days, but other *Southern Living* classics are as popular now as when they first appeared, sometimes in their original form and sometimes updated. Chicken Tetrazzini has long been a favorite "fix-and-freeze" casserole, with Honey-Chicken Salad and Dianne's Southwestern Cornbread Salad among the perennial favorites for ladies' lunches, family reunions, and church suppers.

The most requested *Southern Living* recipe of all time is the Hummingbird Cake, submitted in 1978 by Mrs. L.H. Wiggins of Greensboro, North Carolina. "It just took off and became this iconic recipe that has run in all kinds of food magazines, usually attributed to *Southern Living*," said former Senior Food Editor Mary Allen Perry. "It's like the best banana bread you ever had, made into a layer cake and topped with cream cheese frosting."

Reading the magazine's recipe files not only brings memories of great food but also of great cooks. "I always loved pulling reader recipes out of our files because they'd have notes on them about when the reader served that dish or a story about somebody they loved who had passed the recipe down," said former Executive Food Editor Susan Dosier. "You felt like you knew them. Even today, I can spot a *Southern Living* reader anywhere I go. They love through food. That's how they reach out and get their arms around people—by cooking for them."

Clockwise from top left: Dianne's Southwestern Cornbread Salad (page 304), Tomato-Leek Pie (page 305), and Honey-Chicken Salad (page 304)

Zucchini, Squash, and
Corn Casserole,
page 305

Chicken Tetrazzini,
page 304

"The summer picnic gave the ladies a chance to show off their baking hands. On the barbecue pit, chickens and spareribs sputtered in their own fat and a sauce whose recipe was guarded in the family like a scandalous affair . . ."

—MAYA ANGELOU, AUTHOR,
THE COLLECTED AUTOBIOGRAPHIES OF MAYA ANGELOU

Hummingbird Cake,
page 305

summer
suppers

In the relaxed atmosphere of Amelia Island, two Florida couples host a patio cocktail supper that's gracious, yet summertime easy. It's their favorite way to entertain a large group.

Summer Breezes
Beckon Outdoor Parties

A cool breeze and a deck are reasons enough to entertain outdoors in the summer. You are invited to drop in on parties from the shores of Florida to the heart of Texas and gather an assortment of recipes, menus, and entertaining ideas.

by JEAN WICKSTROM

Once the long, carefree days of summer come, people begin to move their entertaining out-of-doors. Decks, swimming pools, and backyard picnic tables are the settings for many relaxed summer parties. On the following pages, you'll find themes, menus, and recipes as varied as the areas of the South from which they come.

The favorite summertime party of two Florida couples is a lavish patio cocktail supper.

With the relaxed atmosphere of Amelia Island providing the setting, Becky and Dick James and Anne and David Coonrod have found that this type of party is a gracious, yet fun way to entertain a large group of friends.

The menu for the gala occasion reflects Becky and Anne's careful planning. Their selection of dishes combines flavor and variety with simplicity in preparation and serving. Many of the delicacies can be prepared and frozen days before the party. Since fresh seafood is so readily available, both hostesses like to include it in their menu plans.

Colorful party tables are arranged on the James' spacious patio, and guests move from table to table, sampling delightful dishes like Sherried Crab and Shrimp, fried scallops, and marinated asparagus. Dessert is a choice of fresh strawberries and two kinds of cake.

Even though Becky and Anne's menu is extensive, it can be easily adapted to suit your own party plans.

Caviar Dip   Fresh Vegetables
Buttery Cheese Wafers
Marinated Asparagus
Spinach Balls
Creamy Shrimp Remoulade
Fried Scallop Puffs
Crab Fingers With Garlic Butter Sauce
Sherried Crab and Shrimp
Smoked Turkey   Celery Seed Mayonnaise
Fresh Strawberries
Rum Cake
Carrot Loaf Cake
Cocktails   Wine

The tree-canopied patio of the Dick James' home provides a setting as gracious and relaxed as the occasion. Colorful tables are laden with tempting party food, ranging from smoked turkey to rum cake.

CAVIAR DIP

1 (8-ounce) package cream cheese, softened
½ cup mayonnaise
1 cup commercial sour cream
⅛ teaspoon salt
¼ teaspoon red pepper
1 teaspoon Worcestershire sauce
½ teaspoon lemon juice
1 (4-ounce) jar caviar

Combine all ingredients except caviar in container of electric blender; process until smooth. Stir in caviar. Chill; serve with fresh vegetables. Yield: 2½ cups.

BUTTERY CHEESE WAFERS

1 cup butter or margarine, softened
1 pound sharp Cheddar cheese, shredded
2 cups all-purpose flour
1 teaspoon salt
4 or 5 dashes of hot sauce or cayenne pepper
Pecan halves

Combine butter and cheese, cream until smooth. Add remaining ingredients except pecans; mix well with hands. Divide dough in half; form each half into a 13-inch roll. Wrap each in waxed paper; twist ends of waxed paper to seal. Chill 3 to 4 hours.

Cut each roll into ¼-inch slices, and place on greased cookie sheets. Top each slice with 1 pecan half. Bake at 350° for 10 to 12 minutes. (Watch carefully as they brown easily.) Yield: about 10 dozen.

MARINATED ASPARAGUS

3 pounds fresh asparagus
About 1½ cups oil-and-vinegar salad dressing

Break off tough end of each asparagus spear by bending stalk gently until it snaps easily. Wash spears thoroughly in warm water; drain well. Peel stalks with vegetable peeler to remove scales, or peel off tough scales with a knife.

Place asparagus in a shallow baking dish; pour salad dressing over spears. Cover tightly and chill 48 hours, turning asparagus occasionally. Drain well before serving. Yield: about 25 to 30 appetizer servings.

SPINACH BALLS

2 (10-ounce) packages frozen chopped spinach
3 cups herb-seasoned stuffing mix
1 large onion, finely chopped
6 eggs, well beaten
¾ cup melted butter or margarine
½ cup grated Parmesan cheese
1 tablespoon pepper
1½ teaspoons garlic salt
½ teaspoon thyme

Cook spinach according to package directions; drain well, and squeeze to remove excess moisture. Combine spinach and remaining ingredients, mixing well. Shape spinach mixture into ¾-inch balls, and place on lightly greased cookie sheets. Bake at 325° for 15 to 20 minutes. Yield: 11 dozen.

Note: Spinach Balls can be frozen before baking. Place on cookie sheet, and freeze until firm. When frozen, remove from cookie sheet and store in plastic

July 1978　**83**

A LOOK BACK

Food & Fellowship

JULY 1978

The Southern tradition of outdoor gatherings can be attributed to the region's long summer season. Whether it's a garden party or a family cookout, *Southern Living* has always shared summer recipes perfect for keeping the kitchen cool and the conversation lively.

Set for the Season

ATLANTA, GEORGIA

Reindeer candelabra, emerald accents, and mounds of blooms in sugar plum shades infuse this elegant room with holiday magic.

Christmas
Cheer
Is An
Elegant
Table

in these
Birmingham, Atlanta,
Gainesville,
and Lexington homes.

SOUTHERN HOSPITALITY

Here in the South, our distinctive brand of hospitality is like great folk art—it's difficult to define, but we all know it when we see it. Perhaps we can more easily agree on its intended result, which is to make guests feel comfortable and welcome, to serve them delicious food.

"My mother was an incredible cook, with such a sense of generosity and providing for other people—she was the patron saint of graciousness," Birmingham chef Frank Stitt once told *Southern Living*. "She always loved to pull out our nice china and linen. It was beautiful, but not affected or fancy—it was sharing the moment and the good things of life."

Early *Southern Living* hospitality was much more formal than it is today, with matching fine china and silver on the table. Now the magazine doesn't hesitate to mix patterns or to use fine crystal with casual pottery. More important, *Southern Living* encourages readers to be creative and develop their own sense of style.

"I remember a centerpiece one time that was just a paper bag rolled down, lined with a napkin and filled with two mums, French bread, and a bottle of wine," said Judy Feagin, whose entertaining expertise was legendary at *Southern Living*. "And it was gorgeous. You'll entertain more if you realize that you don't have to spend a lot of money, and you don't have to go by all these rules—but you still need to RSVP, arrive on time, and thank your hostess afterward."

Whether you call or send a note of thanks, you should say that the food was delicious, that the table was just beautiful, and that everybody had "the best time." Because that's what every Southern cook wants most of all—good times around the table together.

The Gift of Soul Food

BY APRIL REYNOLDS

AUTHOR OF *KNEE-DEEP IN WONDER*

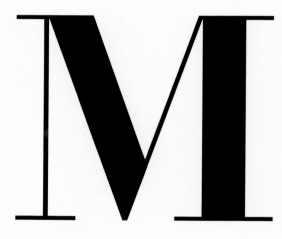

MY MOTHER'S CHITTERLINGS ARE THE STUFF OF LEGEND. At least in my family. Part of their fame is derived from the taste—creamy yet pungent—but my mother's chitterlings are also renowned because of the work involved in making them. For days my sisters and I would stand hunched over the kitchen sink or the bathtub, cleaning a huge bucketful of pig intestines. We then soaked them in cold water and vinegar. Rinse. Repeat. And then our mother would gather together our efforts, add secret ingredients—she still hasn't told anyone her recipe—and a day later our family would eat the best chitterlings outside my grandmother's kitchen in Eastman, Georgia. It was a dish that graced our Thanksgiving and Christmas tables, became the highlight of birthday dinners, was a reward for stellar report cards. I've seen how my mother's soul food bridges divides and makes introductions to Southern culture. I've even seen my mother's chitterlings become a gift, a thank you, and a welcome.

When I was seventeen, I met two Mormon missionaries from the North. I was fascinated by their manner, their accents, their difference. Nowhere was our divide so stark as when it came to food. We all blinked when these two boys spoke of hummus, bagels, lox. "Those poor babies," my mother said. "They never had collard greens or pickled pig's feet?" In fact the list of what those two boys hadn't tasted was so long, my father finally said aloud what we all were thinking: "Well, what do they eat up there?" What, indeed. My mother may not have known a thing about Joseph Smith, but she did know "Those boys need to be eating something real. What with all that walking they do."

Thus began David and Mark's six-month introduction to soul food and Southern hospitality. Soul food is often described as fare prepared by African Americans who predominantly lived in the South. Cheap cuts of meat or vegetables that many would consider weeds were cleverly seasoned. The origin of soul food can be traced back to the slave trade. But in our house, soul food was an everyday dinner. Bits of this, scraps of that, became tasty, hard-won meals. David and Mark came to our house to eat this version of home cooking every other week. Our new friends soon realized there was no shame in asking for second helpings; my mother was suspicious of those who didn't ask for just a bit more. And they really liked the food. Who wouldn't? Smothered pork chops and dirty rice, Brunswick stew and collards studded with smoked ham hocks. After a couple of months, Mark and David asked Mother if they could bring some of their fellow missionaries to dinner. They felt guilty that they were eating too well. I remember my mother throwing her head back with laughter. "Course, now. Those poor babies." Sometimes we had as many as six missionaries over. Young men from Utah, Arizona, Alaska, and as far away as England gathered around our table and ate heaps and second helpings. Their favorite word was, "Wow." "I mean really, wow. That was amazing." "Like that, do you? You come on back." During those exchanges it was hard to figure out who smiled more, my mother or her guests.

Looking back it seemed inevitable where all those dinners would take us. One Wednesday, after Mark finished a third helping of macaroni and cheese, he looked plaintively at my mother and asked, "Could you teach us how to cook like this?" Momma didn't laugh this time; her wry smile spoke a paragraph. "I was wondering when y'all was gone ask." So my mother opened a soul food school for Mormon missionaries, and she taught them how to make gravy, how to clean collard greens, the many uses of dill pickle juice. But most of all my mother taught those young men how to make do. In front of a scantily stocked pantry, she pointed out her bounty. She taught them the essence of soul food: patience and creativity. Good food and hospitality didn't need a fat wallet.

My mother, a Georgia native, had learned from her mother how to make the most out of almost nothing at all. Growing up, we learned from her just what scraps of things with the right spices could be turned into. She taught us the secrets to deviled eggs and my grandmother's fried chicken with pickled jalapeños. There was a culinary world waiting for you if you knew how to properly wield Lawry's Seasoned Salt and pickle juice. She also made sure we learned the fundamentals of cooking: Be careful about throwing anything away, mind the temperature, and trust your tongue. A dab of this, a handful of that, add until you have just enough—mysterious instructions when you hear them. But when standing alongside an expert what is necessary becomes clear. Or as my mother told us, "I'm not telling you to trust me; I'm teaching you how to trust you."

David and Mark's soul food cooking lessons came to a close when their stint as missionaries came to an end. We were all sad to see them go. But my mother had one more surprise. It wasn't Christmas or Thanksgiving, and as far as we knew it wasn't anyone's birthday, but my mother's final meal for those missionaries was a gift all the same. Chitterlings. The ultimate scrap transformed. David and Mark had never heard of them. For a last time, my family and six Mormon missionaries gathered around the table. "You'll remember this," my mother murmured while ladling out what my family considered ambrosia into shallow bowls.

While we ate, it was quiet as church. Then and now, I wonder what those missionaries were thinking as they ate my mother's chitterlings. Were they like me and marveled how soul food was Southern hospitality and culture found in a spoonful? Were they amazed at how a meager but flavorful cuisine could bridge a divide? The hush while we ate made me think these young men realized my mother had given us a gift. She had given us a bit of her soul.

"In our house, soul food was an everyday dinner."

———

SOUTHERN 'CUE

—

How you like it depends on who raised you and where.

Smitty's Market
LOCKHART, TEXAS

In this Texas-style joint,
eager customers line up in a
sooty corridor, and as you get
closer to the cash register,
you are in the smokehouse.

WE ALL LOVE IT, and how we serve it says a lot about where we came from. As Southern gatherings go, a barbecue has no rival. Nothing brings a crowd together like smoky, succulent meat served with the classic sides—baked beans, coleslaw, and potato salad—and gallons of sweet tea. Just about any time of year, with the possible exceptions of Thanksgiving and Christmas, we will happily convene around a red and white checked tablecloth,

preferably one with squeeze bottles of homemade sauce and bowls of dill pickles for a centerpiece.

We appreciate great barbecue for many reasons, not the least of which is our undying respect for pit masters. From the wood that makes the smoke to the rub that flavors the meat, every choice made around the pit matters.

You cannot barbecue quickly. You cannot learn to barbecue quickly. Pit masters are wholly dedicated to the art and craft of it, and when we taste their handiwork, we know we're experiencing a labor of love.

This smoky goodness is also a delightfully democratic cuisine. Wherever you live, the best barbecue in town is the best barbecue in town. Everybody eats there, not only because the food is good, but because it tends to be affordable. Social pretentions go out the window, as we are all made equal by the sauce on our fingers and the bibs beneath our chins.

Barbecue says something about us because the meats and sauces of choice vary dramatically from one region to the next. It's beef in Texas, whole hogs or pork shoulders in the Carolinas, mutton in Kentucky, ribs in Memphis, and all kinds of variations across the South. You could favor a vinegar-based "dip," Alabama white sauce, a thick tomato-based brew, or no sauce at all, depending on where you grew up.

All of these regional styles come together each year at the Memphis in May World Championship Barbecue Cooking Contest. Part of the Memphis in May International Festival, the barbecue contest began in 1978 with 20 teams competing for $1,000 in prize money. Today hundreds of teams, with names like Squeal Street BBQ and The Moody Ques, compete for over $100,000 in prizes.

No matter what part of the South you come from, there's one way you would never eat barbecue: alone. Food this good always brings us together.

BARBECUE PIT MASTERS

The people behind the pits are as compelling as the meat that emerges from them. A diverse group united by a smoky passion, here are some of the South's best.

Ed Mitchell, Raleigh, North Carolina

Chris Lilly, Decatur, Alabama

Will Fleischman, Dallas, Texas

Jack Easley, Marion, Kentucky

Aaron Franklin, Austin, Texas

Francisca Andrin, Chamblee, Georgia

Rodney Scott, Hemingway, South Carolina

Helen Turner, Brownsville, Texas

Sam Jones, Ayden, North Carolina

*"It's just dry rub, patience,
and sauce on the side."*

CHRIS LILLY, PIT MASTER, *SOUTHERN LIVING*, JUNE 2012

Simply Deviled Eggs,
page 309

284

The *Southern Living* Pulled
Pork Sandwich, page 306

BARBECUE IS FOURTH FARE

BY LENA STURGES

Photos by Gil Barrera

In Bee County, Texas, these refinements in barbecuing make for tender, juicy, and crusty well seasoned meats.

Wherever there's smoke on the Fourth, there's bound to be barbecue! Barbecue beef, pork, or chicken might be acclaimed as the official Southern meat dish for the Fourth.

Where food is concerned, no festivity is more popular in the South than the barbecue that's a part of political rallies, family reunions, and special holidays.

There are many versions of the origin of barbecue. Some books say it was derived from the French *barbe a queue,* meaning "beard to tail," which implies cooking the whole animal.

Others favor the Spanish *barbacoa,* derived from a Haitian word meaning "framework of sticks." It was used to describe the outdoor feast of West Indian origin where fish was broiled on irons supported by wooden stakes. About 1700 the barbecue was brought to North America and became popular on plantations of the South as a convenient way of entertaining large numbers.

(Continued on page 47)

39

A LOOK BACK

Fourth Fare

JULY 1967

One of the first issues of *Southern Living* tackled the debate over the origin of barbecue. But there's no argument that we've covered barbecue from all over the region over the years. This particular issue featured 300 pounds of meat cooked by "barbecue chef" Alonzo Blackwell in a pit 10 feet long by 30 inches wide in Bee County, Texas.

The Soul of True Barbecue

BY JANE AND MICHAEL STERN

FOOD, TRAVEL, AND CULTURE WRITERS

Bigg's Place was a barbecue parlor on a gravel road deep in the Arkansas Ozarks. It was a dive. There were no plates; food came on butcher paper. The only utensils were knives attached to the tables with chains long enough for customers to cut their hot links but not each other. To us, it was a taste of heaven. Bigg's coarse-chopped pork—velvet soft with crunchy edges, haloed in hickory, glistening ferociously with exclamatory sauce, and packed into a bun with cool coleslaw—was second to none.

We came across Bigg's Place during our first big eating trip through the South, long ago when few barbecues had their own sauce bottled and ready to sell. We had stocked up on plastic jugs and Tupperware tubs and paid a dollar or two to get them filled whenever we found a place with sauce that we absolutely needed to take home as an edible remembrance of the trip. After an ambrosial Bigg's Place meal, we realized we had run out of containers. We pleaded with Mr. Bigg to somehow pack up some of his magic potion, whereupon he walked out back to a pile of discarded liquor bottles and returned with an emptied fifth of Jack Daniel's. He carefully wiped its neck on his sleeve before filling it.

It kills us to say that we never enjoyed that souvenir sauce, because we lost it on the way home. We were traveling in a station wagon that by the end of the trip was packed with sauces we had collected along the way—dozens of pints and quarts and gallons jammed helter-skelter, floor to roof, from the tailgate to the front seat headrests. Waiting at a red light just north of Myrtle Beach, we were tail-ended by a runaway gravel truck that had lost its brakes. We were okay, as was the truck driver, but the car was totaled; and the sauce we had spent weeks accumulating had splattered all over us and the pavement. Ambulances from four counties converged on what looked like the goriest disaster in highway history. Onlookers were relieved to know that the red stuff everywhere was not blood, but we were disconsolate. The crumpled car was insured; there was no adequate reparation for all the lost sauce.

Our grief will be understood by barbecue devotees, for there is no other food that inspires such passion—a rapturous mix of reverence and hunger-lust. On this subject, the two of us were late to enlightenment. Jane is from New York City, where she grew up thinking that barbecue was spareribs in a Chinese restaurant; and Michael is from the suburban Midwest, where barbecue is a verb that describes the act of roasting weenies on the patio. It wasn't until we visited such smoke-pit meccas as Lexington, North Carolina, and Birmingham, Alabama, that we began to understand barbecue as a noun, referring to meat that is indirectly cooked, low and slow, in a haze of smoke according to rituals that are centuries old.

We also came to believe that not only is barbecue just about the tastiest food on earth; it is a national treasure. Actually, it is many national treasures, because one thing we have learned is how different barbecue is from state to state and plate to plate. Like DNA, no two meals are exactly alike, from chipped mutton with dip and burgoo in western Kentucky to chopped whole hog in eastern North Carolina to mustard-sauced 'cue with hash and rice in South Carolina.

While many of the unique local dishes we seek around the nation are hard to find or scarce to the point of near-extinction (like Indiana persimmon pudding or Yankee red flannel hash), barbecue is easy to locate because it continues to thrive throughout the South. Hunting it is particularly fun because so many purveyors advertise their presence with an unmistakable visual cue: a sign that shows extremely happy pigs. We've got thousands of photos of jolly porkers we have encountered on the road, from the neon piglets who dance on the roof of Bob Sykes' place in Bessemer, Alabama, to the dapper swine in top hat and tails who twirls his walking stick above Leonard's in Memphis. Our favorite is from bygone Harold's of Atlanta. It showed a bespectacled pig cheerfully sitting atop the pile of flaming logs that were cooking him.

Speaking of logs, we must note that many barbecue joints, even some of the most respected, have forsaken the laborious process of burning logs down to coals, then cooking the meat over smoke wafting from the smoldering coals. A gas or electric oven is used, either because local clean-air law now forbids smoke-cooking or simply because a regular oven is easier. But to those of us who prize the real thing, the shortcut method is a misdemeanor, if not a felony. When we pull up to a barbecue joint, there are two things we immediately do. First, we look around for a woodpile. Second, we inhale. No food advertising could possibly be as enticing as the sweet woodsy aroma that pervades a traditional smoke pit.

That distinctive smell keeps eaters honest. It is absolutely impossible to tell your significant other that you had lunch at a salad bar or tell your boss you ate in your cubicle if you've actually been near real barbecue. All the Febreze in the world will not camouflage its scent, which clings tenaciously to clothes, hair, and skin like porky Chanel No. 5. A couple decades ago, we interviewed pit master Tony Willett at the glorious Peak Bros. Bar-B-Que Restaurant in Waverly, Kentucky. The pit door was open and Willett was busy throwing spice on pork ribs and turning briskets and hunks of lamb on the grate. Hellish heat and blinding puffs of smoke emanating from the pit didn't bother him at all, but our eyes teared and our glasses fogged. "When I walk into a store, you can hear people say, 'Here comes Peak Brothers!'" Willet confided, "When I go home, my wife makes me stay outside until I take off my clothes." Twenty years after interviewing him, we still can sniff the tantalizing perfume of Peak Bros. on the pages of the notepad we used that day.

"The only utensils were knives attached to the tables with chains long enough for customers to cut their hot links but not each other."

——

THE RECIPES

—

Southern Living *has always been dedicated to bringing readers the food that reflects the South.*

SIGNATURE SOUTHERN

BROWN SUGAR-BOURBON-GLAZED HAM

Choose a bone-in half-ham brined with natural juices. Leaving a thin layer of fat after trimming amps up the flavor and keeps the meat moist.

- 1 (6- to 8-lb.) fully cooked, bone-in ham
- 48 whole cloves
- 1 (16-oz.) package light brown sugar
- 1 cup spicy brown mustard
- 1 cup cola soft drink
- ¾ cup bourbon

1. Preheat oven to 350°. Remove skin from ham, and trim fat to ¼-inch thickness. Make shallow cuts in fat ¾ inch apart in a diamond pattern.

2. Insert cloves in centers of diamonds. Place ham in a lightly greased 13- x 9-inch pan. Stir together brown sugar and next 3 ingredients; spoon mixture over ham.

3. Bake at 350° on lowest oven rack 2 hours and 30 minutes, basting slowly with pan juices every 15 to 20 minutes. Remove ham from oven; let stand 20 minutes before slicing, basting occasionally with pan juices.

MAKES 8 to 10 servings
HANDS-ON 30 min.; **TOTAL** 3 hours, 20 min.

OUR BEST SOUTHERN FRIED CHICKEN

Look no further for that perfect fried chicken recipe. Southerners will find this favorite to be a mouthwatering treasure that they will return to again and again.

- 1 Tbsp. table salt
- 1 (2- to 2½-lb.) whole chicken, cut up
- 1 tsp. table salt
- 1 tsp. freshly ground black pepper
- 1 cup all-purpose flour
- 2 cups vegetable oil
- ¼ cup bacon drippings

1. Combine 3 qt. water and 1 Tbsp. salt in a large bowl; add chicken. Cover and chill 8 hours. Drain chicken; rinse with cold water, and pat dry.

2. Combine 1 tsp. salt and pepper; sprinkle half of pepper mixture over chicken. Combine remaining pepper mixture and flour in a large zip-top plastic freezer bag. Place 2 pieces of chicken in bag. Seal and shake to coat evenly. Remove chicken, and repeat procedure with remaining chicken.

3. Combine vegetable oil and bacon drippings in a 12-inch cast-iron skillet or chicken fryer; heat to 360°. Add chicken, a few pieces at a time, skin side down. Cover and cook 6 minutes; uncover and cook 9 minutes.

4. Turn chicken pieces; cover and cook 6 minutes. Uncover and cook 5 to 9 minutes, turning pieces during last 3 minutes for even browning, if necessary. Drain on paper towels.

Note: For best results, keep the oil temperature between 300° to 325° as you fry the chicken. Also, you may substitute 2 cups buttermilk for the saltwater solution used to brine the chicken pieces. Proceed as directed.

MAKES 4 servings
HANDS-ON 55 min.; **TOTAL** 8 hours, 55 min.

PICKLED SHRIMP WITH FENNEL

Marinated plump shrimp and crunchy sliced fennel make a stellar appetizer and an even better no-fuss cold salad.

- 1 small fennel bulb
- 1 Tbsp. kosher salt
- 2 lb. large raw shrimp, peeled and deveined
- 1 cup fresh lemon juice
- ½ cup white wine vinegar
- 1 small serrano or bird pepper, seeded and thinly sliced
- 1½ tsp. kosher salt
- 1 tsp. sugar
- 1 cup thinly sliced white onion

1. Slice fennel bulb thinly, reserving fronds. Chop fronds to equal 1 Tbsp. Fill a large bowl halfway with ice and water.

2. Bring 1 Tbsp. kosher salt and 2 qt. water to a boil in a Dutch oven over high heat. Remove from heat; add shrimp, and let stand, stirring once, 1 minute or just until shrimp turn pink.

3. Transfer shrimp to ice water, using a slotted spoon. Reserve 2 cups hot cooking liquid in a medium bowl. Let shrimp stand 10 minutes, stirring once. Transfer shrimp to a paper towel-lined plate, reserving ice water in bowl.

4. Whisk lemon juice and next 4 ingredients into reserved hot cooking liquid until salt and sugar dissolve. Place bowl in reserved ice water, and whisk lemon juice mixture until cooled to room temperature (about 10 minutes).

5. Remove lemon juice mixture from ice water and discard ice water, reserving chilled bowl for shrimp. Stir together onion, fennel slices, chopped fennel fronds, and shrimp in chilled bowl. Pour cooled lemon juice mixture over shrimp mixture. Cover and chill 1 hour to 2 days. Serve with a slotted spoon.

MAKES 8 servings
HANDS-ON 30 min., **TOTAL** 2 hours

PIMIENTO CHEESE

This pimiento cheese delivers herby flavor from fresh parsley and dill. Pepperoncini peppers and horseradish give the cheese mixture of sharp Cheddar and Havarti added kick.

- 1 (12-oz.) jar roasted red bell peppers, drained and finely chopped
- 1 cup mayonnaise
- ¼ cup finely chopped red onion
- ¼ cup chopped fresh parsley
- 1 Tbsp. chopped fresh dill
- 2 Tbsp. Dijon mustard
- 2 Tbsp. chopped jarred pepperoncini salad peppers
- 1 Tbsp. liquid from pepperoncini peppers
- 1 tsp. grated fresh horseradish
- 4 cups (16 oz.) shredded sharp Cheddar cheese
- 3 cups (12 oz.) shredded Havarti cheese

Stir together roasted red bell peppers, mayonnaise, red onion, parsley, dill, Dijon mustard, chopped pepperoncini peppers, liquid from peppers, and horseradish. Gently stir in Cheddar cheese and Havarti cheese until well blended. Cover and chill until ready to serve.

MAKES 6 cups
HANDS-ON 25 min., **TOTAL** 25 min.

THE ULTIMATE CLASSIC COLLARDS

Tangy vinegar brightens the earthy flavors, and a touch of honey rounds out the smoke from the ham hock.

- 3 (1-lb.) packages fresh collard greens
- 12 smoked bacon slices, chopped
- 2 medium-size yellow onions, chopped
- 3 garlic cloves, minced
- 3 cups reduced-sodium fat-free chicken broth
- ¼ cup apple cider vinegar
- 2 Tbsp. honey
- 1 (12- to 16-oz.) smoked ham hock
  Kosher salt
  Freshly ground black pepper

Remove and chop collard stems. Chop collard leaves. Cook bacon in a large Dutch oven over medium heat, stirring occasionally, 12 to 15 minutes or until just crisp. Add onion, and sauté 8 minutes or until onion is tender. Add garlic; sauté 1 minute. Stir in chicken broth and next 2 ingredients; add ham hock. Increase heat to high, and bring to a boil. Add collards in batches. Reduce heat to medium-low; cover and cook 2 hours or until desired tenderness. Remove meat from ham hock, and chop; discard bone. Stir chopped meat into collards. Season with kosher salt and freshly ground pepper.

MAKES 6 to 8 servings
HANDS-ON 50 min.; **TOTAL** 2 hours, 50 min.

PERFECT POT OF GRITS

2 tsp. kosher salt
1 cup uncooked stone-ground grits
2½ Tbsp. butter

1. Bring salt and 1 qt. water to a boil in a heavy saucepan over high heat. Whisk in grits, and cook, whisking constantly, 45 seconds. Scrape bottom and sides of the pot.

2. Return to a boil; cover. Reduce heat to medium-low. Cook 20 to 25 minutes or until tender. (For a looser consistency, whisk in 2 to 4 Tbsp. water halfway through cooking.)

3. Stir in butter until melted, and serve immediately.

MAKES 4 to 6 servings
HANDS-ON 5 min., **TOTAL** 30 min.

CHICKEN-AND-SAUSAGE GUMBO

A symbol of Creole cooking, hearty gumbo is ubiquitous in homes and restaurants across Louisiana. Andouille sausage and filé powder make our chicken-and-sausage gumbo a classic. As in any good gumbo, a deep, rich roux thickens the stew.

1 lb. andouille sausage, cut into ¼-inch-thick slices
4 skinned bone-in chicken breasts
Vegetable oil
¾ cup all-purpose flour
1 medium onion, chopped
½ green bell pepper, chopped
2 celery ribs, sliced
2 qt. hot water
3 garlic cloves, minced
2 bay leaves
1 Tbsp. Worcestershire sauce
2 tsp. Creole seasoning
½ tsp. dried thyme
½ to 1 tsp. hot sauce
4 green onions, sliced
Filé powder (optional)
Hot cooked rice
Garnish: chopped green onions

1. Cook sausage in a Dutch oven over medium heat, stirring constantly, 5 minutes or until browned. Drain on paper towels; reserve drippings in Dutch oven. Set sausage aside.

2. Cook chicken in reserved drippings in Dutch oven over medium heat 5 minutes or until browned. Drain on paper towels; reserve drippings in Dutch oven. Set chicken aside.

3. Add enough vegetable oil to drippings in Dutch oven to measure ½ cup. Add flour, and cook over medium heat, stirring constantly, 20 to 25 minutes, or until roux is chocolate colored.

4. Stir in onion, bell pepper, and celery, and cook, stirring often, 8 minutes or until tender. Gradually add 2 qt. hot water, and bring mixture to a boil; add chicken, garlic, and next 5 ingredients. Reduce heat to low, and simmer, stirring occasionally, 1 hour. Remove chicken; cool.

5. Add sausage to gumbo; cook 30 minutes. Stir in sliced green onions; cook 30 more minutes.

6. Bone chicken, and cut meat into strips; return chicken to gumbo, and simmer 5 minutes. Remove and discard bay leaves.

7. Remove gumbo from heat. Sprinkle with filé powder, if desired. Serve over hot cooked rice.

MAKES 4 to 6 servings
HANDS-ON 1 hour, 55 min.; **TOTAL** 3 hours

GRANNIE'S CRACKLIN' CORNBREAD

A true classic, our traditional Southern cornbread calls for just six ingredients.

¼ cup butter
2 cups self-rising cornmeal mix
½ cup all-purpose flour
2½ cups buttermilk
2 large eggs, lightly beaten
1 cup cracklings*

1. Preheat oven to 425°. Place butter in a 9-inch cast-iron skillet, and heat in oven 4 minutes.

2. Combine cornmeal and flour in a large bowl; make a well in center of mixture.

3. Stir together buttermilk, eggs, and cracklings; add to dry ingredients, stirring just until moistened. Pour over melted butter in hot skillet.

4. Bake at 425° for 25 to 30 minutes or until golden brown.

MAKES 8 to 10 servings
HANDS-ON 7 min., **TOTAL** 37 min.

*1 cup cooked, crumbled bacon (12 to 15 slices) may be substituted for cracklings.

Grannie's Cracklin' Cakes: Prepare batter as directed above; stir in ¼ cup butter, melted. Heat a large skillet coated with vegetable cooking spray over medium-high heat. Spoon about ¼ cup batter for each cake into skillet; cook, in batches, 2 to 3 minutes on each side or until golden.

OUR FAVORITE BUTTERMILK BISCUIT

After baking hundreds of biscuits, our Test Kitchen landed on this winning recipe for our favorite. This no-fail biscuit recipe will impress new cooks and old pros alike.

- ½ cup butter, frozen
- 2 ½ cups self-rising flour
- 1 cup chilled buttermilk
  Parchment paper
- 2 Tbsp. butter, melted

1. Preheat oven to 475°. Grate frozen butter using large holes of a box grater. Toss grated butter and flour together in a medium bowl. Chill 10 minutes.

2. Make a well in center of mixture. Add buttermilk, and stir 15 times. (Dough will be sticky.)

3. Turn dough out onto a lightly floured surface. Lightly sprinkle flour over top of dough. Using a lightly floured rolling pin, roll dough into a ¾-inch-thick rectangle (about 9 x 5 inches). Fold dough in half so short ends meet. Repeat rolling and folding process 4 more times.

4. Roll dough to ½-inch thickness. Cut with a 2 ½-inch floured round cutter, reshaping scraps and flouring as needed.

5. Place dough rounds on a parchment paper-lined jelly-roll pan. Bake at 475° for 15 minutes or until lightly browned. Brush with melted butter.

MAKES 12 to 14 biscuits
HANDS-ON 25 min., TOTAL 50 min.

For Pillowy Dinner Rolls: Cut in ½ cup cold shortening instead of cold butter. You'll get a soft biscuit that stays tender, even when cool. Plus, shortening has a neutral flavor that complements anything on your dinner plate.

For Sweet Shortcakes: Add 2 Tbsp. sugar to the flour, and replace buttermilk with heavy cream. The sugar lends the biscuits a subtle sweetness, and the extra fat in heavy cream gives them a crumbly texture like shortbread. They are the perfect base for shortcake desserts.

For Crunchy-Bottomed Biscuits: Warm a cast-iron skillet in the oven, and spread a bit of butter in the skillet before adding the biscuits. The bottoms will end up crunchy and golden brown and provide a sturdy base to hold up to a smothering of sausage gravy for a hearty breakfast.

For Pickle Biscuits: Why didn't we think of these sooner? Stir 4 Tbsp. drained dill pickle relish into buttermilk before adding to flour mixture. Split baked biscuits, and top with ham and mustard for the World's Best Ham Sandwich! We promise.

BASIC WHITE CAKE WITH PEPPERMINT FROSTING

- 1 cup butter, softened
- 2 cups sugar
- 1 Tbsp. loosely packed orange zest
- 1 tsp. vanilla extract
- 3 ½ cups all-purpose flour
- 1 Tbsp. baking powder
- ¼ tsp. table salt
- 1 cup milk
- 8 large egg whites
  Shortening
  Peppermint Frosting

1. Preheat oven to 325°. Beat butter at medium speed with an electric stand mixer until creamy. Gradually add sugar, beating until light and fluffy. Add orange zest and vanilla; beat until blended. Combine flour and next 2 ingredients; add to butter mixture alternately with milk, beginning and ending with flour mixture. Beat at low speed just until blended after each addition.

2. Beat egg whites at high speed until stiff peaks form. Stir egg whites into batter in 3 batches. Spoon into 3 greased (with shortening) and floured 9-inch round cake pans.

3. Bake at 325° for 25 minutes or until a wooden pick inserted in center comes out clean. Cool in pans on wire racks 10 minutes; remove from pans to wire racks, and cool completely (about 1 hour).

4. Place 1 Basic White Cake layer on a serving platter. Spread 1 cup peppermint candy frosting mixture over cake layer. Top with second layer, and spread remaining 1 cup peppermint candy frosting over cake layer. Top with third cake layer, and spread top and sides of cake with remaining plain Peppermint Frosting. Sprinkle with remaining crushed candies, or top with a fondant bow. (See page 298.)

Note: Cake layers may be baked in 3 (8-inch) square disposable aluminum foil pans. Increase bake time to 26 to 30 minutes.

MAKES 10 to 12 servings
HANDS-ON 30 min.; TOTAL 2 hours, 45 min.

PEPPERMINT FROSTING

- 1 cup butter, softened
- 1 (8-oz. package) cream cheese, softened
- ¼ tsp. table salt
- 1 tsp. vanilla extract
- ½ tsp. peppermint extract
- 1 (32-oz.) package powdered sugar
- 2 to 3 Tbsp. milk
- 12 hard peppermint candies

1. Beat first 3 ingredients at medium speed with an electric mixer until creamy. Beat in extracts. Gradually add powdered sugar alternately with 2 Tbsp. milk. Beat at low speed until blended and smooth after each addition. Add up to 1 Tbsp. milk, 1 tsp. at a time, beating until frosting reaches desired consistency.

2. Reserve 2 cups frosting in a small bowl. Process peppermint candies in a food processor until finely crushed. Stir ¼ cup crushed candies into reserved 2 cups frosting.

PEPPERMINT FONDANT BOW

For the bow, buy 1 lb. each of red and white rolled fondant from the cake section of a crafts store. Roll a thin red strip, and follow our steps below for the bow. Dust your countertop with cornstarch or powdered sugar to prevent sticking.

ROLL LONG STRIPS

You need a rolling pin, pizza wheel, ruler, and red and white fondant. Roll a chunk of red and chunk of white fondant into two long strips (about ⅛ inch thick). Using ruler and pizza wheel, cut white fondant into thin strips.

MAKE STRIPED RIBBON

Moisten finger with water; rub one side of one thin white strip. Place strip, moist side down, on red to form a stripe. Repeat with two to three white strips. Roll gently with rolling pin. Repeat as needed to make more ribbons.

CUT, SHAPE, DRY

Cut two identical ribbons for tails. Place foil under tails to create folds. Form loops of bow by wrapping ribbon around a cardboard roll, leaving ¼ inch excess on ends. Pinch ends. Cut a small rectangle for knot. Let dry 24 hours.

ASSEMBLE BOW

Place bow tails on cake, draping down sides. Place bow loops over ribbon on top of cake (loop ends touching). Tip loops at an angle, and press gently into frosting to secure. Cover seam with knot, using frosting as glue, if needed.

KEY LIME POUND CAKE

- 1 cup butter, softened
- ½ cup shortening
- 3 cups sugar
- 6 large eggs
- 3 cups all-purpose flour
- ½ tsp. baking powder
- ⅛ tsp. table salt
- 1 cup milk
- 1 tsp. vanilla extract
- 1 tsp. lime zest
- ¼ cup fresh Key lime juice
  Key Lime Glaze
  Garnishes: lime slices, whipped cream, fresh mint

1. Preheat oven to 325°. Beat butter and shortening at medium speed with a heavy-duty electric stand mixer 2 to 3 minutes or until creamy. Gradually add sugar, beating 5 to 7 minutes. Add eggs, 1 at a time, beating just until yellow disappears.

2. Combine flour, baking powder, and salt. Add to butter mixture alternately with milk, beginning and ending with flour mixture. Beat at low speed just until blended after each addition. Stir in vanilla, lime zest, and lime juice. Pour batter into a greased and floured 10-inch (12-cup) tube pan.

3. Bake at 325° for 1 hour and 15 minutes to 1 hour and 20 minutes or until a long wooden pick inserted in center comes out clean. Cool in pan on a wire rack 10 to 15 minutes; remove from pan to a wire rack.

4. Meanwhile, make Key Lime Glaze. Immediately brush over top and sides of cake. Cool completely (about 1 hour).

MAKES 12 servings
HANDS-ON 30 min., **TOTAL** 2 hours

KEY LIME GLAZE

- 1 cup powdered sugar
- 2 Tbsp. fresh Key lime juice
- ½ tsp. vanilla extract

Whisk together powdered sugar, fresh Key lime juice, and vanilla until smooth. Use immediately.

MAKES ½ cup
HANDS-ON 5 min., **TOTAL** 5 min.

Key Lime Pound Cake

FARM TO TABLE

HEIRLOOM TOMATO SALAD

ROASTED SWEET POTATO-
AND-ONION TART

TENNESSEE WHISKEY-PECAN PIE

MINTY LEMONADE

KALE-AND-BLUEBERRY SLAW WITH
BUTTERMILK DRESSING

CREAMY BASIL-BLACK
PEPPER CUCUMBERS

CUCUMBERS WITH GINGER,
RICE VINEGAR, AND MINT

SPINACH-AND-THREE-HERB PESTO

HEIRLOOM TOMATO SALAD

Colorful and flavorful is the best way to describe Heirloom Tomato Salad. Let this eye-catching side adorn your table at your next cookout.

- 4 lb. assorted heirloom tomatoes
- 2 small Kirby cucumbers, sliced
- 1 small red onion, halved and sliced
  Lady Pea Salsa
  Fresh basil leaves

Cut tomatoes into wedges or in half, depending on size. Gently toss tomatoes with cucumbers and onion. Top with Lady Pea Salsa and basil.

MAKES 8 servings
HANDS-ON 15 min.; **TOTAL** 50 min., including salsa

LADY PEA SALSA

Fresh salsa makes a delicious topping for sliced tomatoes, grilled chicken, or steak.

- 1 cup diced unpeeled nectarine
- 2 jalapeño peppers, seeded and minced
- 1 Tbsp. sugar
- 3 Tbsp. fresh lime juice
- 2 tsp. orange zest
- 2 tsp. grated fresh ginger
- 2 cups cooked fresh lady peas
- ½ cup chopped fresh cilantro
- ⅓ cup diced red onion

Stir together first 6 ingredients in a large bowl; let stand 15 minutes. Add peas and next 2 ingredients, and gently toss to coat. Serve immediately, or cover and chill up to 24 hours.

MAKES about 4 cups
HANDS-ON 20 min., **TOTAL** 35 min.

ROASTED SWEET POTATO-AND-ONION TART

- 3 cups (¾-inch-cubed) sweet potatoes (about 1 ½ lb.)
- 1 cup chopped red onion
- 2 Tbsp. olive oil
- 1 tsp. seasoned pepper
- 6 cooked bacon slices, crumbled
- ¼ cup chopped fresh flat-leaf parsley
- 1 (14.1-oz.) package refrigerated piecrusts
- 2 cups (8 oz.) shredded Gruyère cheese
- 1½ cups half-and-half
- 4 large eggs
- 1 tsp. chopped fresh rosemary
- ½ tsp. table salt
  Garnish: fresh rosemary sprig

1. Preheat oven to 425°. Toss first 4 ingredients together in a large bowl; arrange mixture in a single layer in a lightly greased 15- x 10-inch jelly-roll pan. Bake 20 minutes or just until potatoes are tender, stirring after 10 minutes. Cool completely in pan on a wire rack (about 30 minutes). Stir in bacon and chopped parsley.

2. Meanwhile, unroll piecrusts; stack on a lightly greased surface. Roll stacked piecrusts into a 12-inch circle. Fit piecrust into a 10-inch deep-dish tart pan with removable bottom; press into fluted edges. Trim off excess piecrust along edges. Line piecrust with aluminum foil or parchment paper, and fill with pie weights or dried beans. Place pan on a foil-lined baking sheet.

3. Bake at 425° for 12 minutes. Remove weights and foil; bake 5 more minutes. Cool completely on baking sheet on a wire rack (about 15 minutes). Reduce oven temperature to 350°.

4. Layer half of sweet potato mixture and half of cheese in tart shell; repeat layers once.

5. Whisk together half-and-half and eggs; stir in next 2 ingredients; pour over cheese.

6. Bake at 350° on lowest rack 35 to 40 minutes or until set. Cool tart on baking sheet on wire rack 15 minutes. Garnish with rosemary sprig.

MAKES 6 to 8 servings
HANDS-ON 30 min.; **TOTAL** 2 hours, 40 min.

TENNESSEE WHISKEY-PECAN PIE

We love the combination of pecans and smoky-sweet bourbon in the thick, rich pie filling. For a booze-free pie, substitute apple juice for the whiskey in the filling, and serve with plain sweetened whipped cream or enjoy it without.

CRUST
- ½ Tbsp. butter
- ¼ cup finely chopped pecans
- Pinch of kosher salt
- 1 ¼ cups all-purpose flour
- 2 Tbsp. granulated sugar
- ½ tsp. table salt
- ¼ cup cold butter, cubed
- ¼ cup cold shortening, cubed
- 3 to 4 Tbsp. buttermilk

FILLING
- 1 cup dark corn syrup
- ½ cup granulated sugar
- ½ cup firmly packed light brown sugar
- ¼ cup Tennessee whiskey*
- 4 large eggs
- ¼ cup butter, melted
- 2 tsp. plain white cornmeal
- 2 tsp. vanilla extract
- ½ tsp. table salt
- 2 ½ cups lightly toasted pecan halves

REMAINING INGREDIENTS
- Vegetable cooking spray
- Whiskey Whipped Cream (optional)

1. Prepare Crust: Melt ½ Tbsp. butter in a small skillet over medium heat, swirling to coat sides of pan. Add ¼ cup finely chopped pecans, and sauté 2 minutes or until fragrant and lightly toasted. Sprinkle pecan mixture with a pinch of salt. Remove pecans from skillet, and cool completely. Reserve for use in Step 4.

2. Pulse flour and next 2 ingredients in a food processor 3 or 4 times or until well combined. Add cubed cold butter and cold shortening; pulse until mixture resembles coarse meal. Drizzle 3 Tbsp. buttermilk over flour mixture, and pulse just until moist clumps form. (Add up to 1 Tbsp. buttermilk, 1 tsp. at a time, if necessary.) Shape dough into a flat disk, and wrap tightly with plastic wrap. Chill dough at least 1 hour.

3. Meanwhile, prepare Filling: Place corn syrup and next 3 ingredients in a large saucepan, and bring to a boil over medium heat, whisking constantly. Cook, whisking constantly, 2 minutes; remove from heat. Whisk together eggs and next 4 ingredients in a bowl. Gradually whisk about one-fourth of hot corn syrup mixture into egg mixture; gradually add egg mixture to remaining corn syrup mixture, whisking constantly. Stir in 2 ½ cups lightly toasted pecan halves; cool completely (about 30 minutes).

4. Preheat oven to 325°. Unwrap dough, and roll into a 13-inch circle on a lightly floured surface. Sprinkle dough with sautéed pecans (reserved from Step 1). Place a piece of plastic wrap over dough and pecans, and lightly roll pecans into dough. Fit dough into a lightly greased (with cooking spray) 9-inch pie plate. Fold edges under, and crimp. Pour cooled filling into prepared crust.

5. Bake at 325° for 50 to 55 minutes or until set; cool pie completely on a wire rack (about 2 hours) before slicing. Serve with Whiskey Whipped Cream, if desired.

*Water or apple juice may be substituted.

Note: We tested with Jack Daniel's whiskey.

MAKES 8 servings
HANDS-ON 30 min.; **TOTAL** 3 hours, 10 min.

WHISKEY WHIPPED CREAM

Beat 1 cup heavy cream and 1 tsp. Tennessee whiskey at medium-high speed with an electric mixer until foamy. Gradually add 3 Tbsp. powdered sugar, beating until soft peaks form.

MAKES about 1 ½ cups
HANDS-ON 5 min., **TOTAL** 5 min.

MINTY LEMONADE

Transform lemonade in seconds with a handful of fresh mint leaves. Don't chop them—keep leaves whole to avoid murky lemonade (and bits of green in your teeth). To maximize the mint flavor, cup the leaves in the palm of one hand, and clap your hands together to release the herb's aroma.

- **Lemonade**
- **Whole fresh mint leaves**

Combine lemonade and mint leaves in a pitcher. Chill until ready to serve.

.

Kale-and-Blueberry Slaw
with Buttermilk Dressing

KALE-AND-BLUEBERRY SLAW WITH BUTTERMILK DRESSING

We like fresh tarragon in this creamy, zippy dressing, but other herbs work just as well.

- 6 Tbsp. apple cider vinegar
- 3 Tbsp. grated onion
- ½ tsp. Worcestershire sauce
- ¼ tsp. hot sauce (such as Tabasco)
- 1 garlic clove, minced
- ½ Granny Smith apple, grated
- 1 cup buttermilk
- 6 Tbsp. mayonnaise
- 6 Tbsp. sour cream
- 3 Tbsp. finely chopped fresh tarragon
- ½ to 1 tsp. kosher salt
- ¼ to ½ tsp. freshly ground black pepper
- ¼ to ½ tsp. sugar
- 6 radishes, thinly sliced
- 4 medium carrots, cut into thin strips
- 1 bunch kale, trimmed and thinly sliced
- ½ small head red cabbage, shredded
- 1 cup fresh blueberries
- 1 cup fresh raspberries

1. Stir together first 6 ingredients in a jar with a tight-fitting lid; let stand 5 minutes. Add buttermilk and next 3 ingredients. Cover jar with lid; shake vigorously until blended and smooth. Add salt, pepper, and sugar to taste.

2. Toss radishes, next 5 ingredients, and ½ cup dressing together in a large bowl; let stand 30 minutes. Season with salt and pepper. Serve with remaining dressing.

MAKES 6 servings
HANDS-ON 30 min.; **TOTAL** 1 hour, 5 min.

CREAMY BASIL-BLACK PEPPER CUCUMBERS

- 2 ½ lb. cucumbers, peeled and cut into spears
- 1 ½ tsp. kosher salt
- ½ cup Greek yogurt
- 3 Tbsp. extra virgin olive oil
- 1 tsp. lime zest
- 2 Tbsp. fresh lime juice
- 1 tsp. freshly ground black pepper
- ½ cup firmly packed fresh basil leaves, chopped
  Garnish: lime peel strips

Toss together cucumbers and salt in a large bowl, and let stand 5 minutes. Whisk together yogurt and next 4 ingredients; gently stir into cucumber mixture. Cover and chill 1 to 24 hours. Add basil, and toss to combine. Let stand 10 minutes before serving. Season with salt.

MAKES 8 servings
HANDS-ON 15 min.; **TOTAL** 1 hour, 30 min.

CUCUMBERS WITH GINGER, RICE VINEGAR, AND MINT

- 2 ½ lb. cucumbers, chopped
- 1 ½ tsp. kosher salt
- ½ cup rice vinegar
- 1 ½ tsp. fresh ginger, minced
- 2 garlic cloves, minced
- ¼ tsp. dried crushed red pepper
- ¼ cup loosely packed fresh mint leaves, chopped
  Freshly ground black pepper

Toss together cucumbers and salt in a large bowl; let stand 5 minutes. Whisk together vinegar and next 3 ingredients. Pour over cucumber mixture; cover and chill 1 to 24 hours. Add mint, and toss to combine. Let stand 10 minutes before serving. Season with salt and pepper.

MAKES 8 servings
HANDS-ON 15 min.; **TOTAL** 1 hour, 20 min.

SPINACH-AND-THREE-HERB PESTO

Versatile pesto tastes great on grilled bread and hard-cooked eggs. Or toss a spoonful with your favorite pasta.

- 1 ⅓ cups grated Parmesan cheese
- 1 cup firmly packed fresh baby spinach
- ⅔ cup olive oil
- ½ cup firmly packed fresh basil leaves
- ¼ cup firmly packed fresh flat-leaf parsley
- ¼ cup chopped toasted pecans
- 3 Tbsp. cold water
- 1 Tbsp. fresh lemon juice
- 1 Tbsp. fresh tarragon leaves
- 2 garlic cloves, chopped
- ¾ tsp. kosher salt

Process all ingredients in a food processor until smooth, stopping to scrape down sides as needed.

MAKES about 1 ½ cups
HANDS-ON 10 min., **TOTAL** 10 min.

COMMUNITY COOKBOOK

CHICKEN TETRAZZINI

HONEY-CHICKEN SALAD

DIANNE'S SOUTHWESTERN
CORNBREAD SALAD

TOMATO-LEEK PIE

ZUCCHINI, SQUASH, AND
CORN CASSEROLE

HUMMINGBIRD CAKE

CHICKEN TETRAZZINI

- 3 Tbsp. butter
- 1 medium onion, chopped
- 1 green bell pepper, chopped
- 1 garlic clove, pressed
- 3 Tbsp. all-purpose flour
- 2 cups milk
- 7 oz. spaghetti, cooked
- 3 cups chopped cooked chicken
- 1 cup (4 oz.) shredded Cheddar cheese, divided
- 1 (10 ¾-oz.) can cream of mushroom soup
- ¼ cup dry white wine
- 1 (4-oz.) can sliced mushrooms, drained
- 1 (2-oz.) jar diced pimiento, drained
- ½ cup grated Parmesan cheese
- 2 Tbsp. chopped fresh parsley
- 1 tsp. table salt
- ½ tsp. freshly ground black pepper

1. Preheat oven to 350°. Melt butter in a large skillet over medium heat; add onion, bell pepper, and garlic. Sauté until tender.

2. Stir in flour; cook, stirring constantly, 1 minute. Gradually stir in milk; cook over medium heat, stirring constantly, until thickened and bubbly.

3. Stir in pasta, chicken, ¾ cup Cheddar cheese, and next 8 ingredients. Spoon mixture into a lightly greased shallow 2-qt. baking dish.

4. Bake at 350° for 20 minutes; sprinkle evenly with remaining ¼ cup Cheddar cheese, and bake 5 more minutes.

MAKES 4 to 6 servings
HANDS-ON 35 min., **TOTAL** 1 hour

Note: To make ahead, prepare as directed; cover and chill. Let stand 30 minutes, uncovered, and bake 35 minutes or until casserole is thoroughly heated.

HONEY-CHICKEN SALAD

- 4 cups chopped cooked chicken
- 3 celery ribs, diced (about 1½ cups)
- 1 cup sweetened dried cranberries
- ½ cup chopped pecans, toasted
- 1½ cups mayonnaise
- ⅓ cup honey
- ¼ tsp. table salt
- ¼ tsp. freshly ground black pepper
  Garnish: chopped toasted pecans

1. Combine first 4 ingredients.

2. Whisk together mayonnaise and next 3 ingredients. Add to chicken mixture, stirring gently until combined.

MAKES 4 to 6 servings
HANDS-ON 20 min., **TOTAL** 20 min.

DIANNE'S SOUTHWESTERN CORNBREAD SALAD

Our standout cornbread salad is a great dish for summer entertaining.

- 1 (6-oz.) package Mexican cornbread mix
- 1 (1-oz.) envelope buttermilk Ranch salad dressing mix
- 1 small head romaine lettuce, shredded
- 2 large tomatoes, chopped
- 1 (15-oz.) can black beans, drained and rinsed
- 1 (15¼-oz.) can whole kernel corn with red and green peppers, drained
- 1 (8-oz.) package shredded Mexican four-cheese blend
- 6 bacon slices, cooked and crumbled
- 5 green onions, chopped

1. Prepare cornbread mix according to package directions; cool and crumble. Set aside.

2. Prepare salad dressing mix according to package directions.

3. Layer a large bowl with half each of cornbread, lettuce, and next 6 ingredients; spoon half of dressing evenly over top. Repeat with remaining ingredients and dressing. Cover and chill at least 2 hours.

MAKES 10 to 12 servings
HANDS-ON 30 min.; **TOTAL** 2 hours, 30 min.

TOMATO-LEEK PIE

─────

- ½ (14.1-oz.) package refrigerated piecrusts
- 2 medium-size red tomatoes
- 2 medium-size yellow tomatoes
- 1 green tomato
- ½ tsp. kosher salt
- 1 medium leek
- 2 Tbsp. butter
- ¼ tsp. freshly ground black pepper
- ½ cup grated Parmesan cheese
- ½ cup light mayonnaise
- 1 large egg, lightly beaten

1. Preheat oven to 450°. Fit piecrust into a 9-inch pie plate according to package directions; fold edges under, and crimp.

2. Bake at 450° for 8 to 10 minutes or until golden brown. Remove from oven, and cool 5 minutes. Reduce oven temperature to 375°.

3. Cut tomatoes into ¼-inch slices. Place tomatoes on a paper towel-lined wire rack. Sprinkle tomatoes with kosher salt. Let stand 20 minutes. Pat dry with paper towels.

4. Remove and discard root and dark green top of leek. Halve lengthwise, and rinse thoroughly under cold running water to remove grit and sand. Thinly slice leek.

5. Melt butter in a large skillet over medium heat; add leek, and sauté 3 to 5 minutes or until tender.

6. Layer leek on bottom of prepared crust. Top with tomato slices, and sprinkle with pepper. Stir together cheese, mayonnaise, and egg in a medium bowl until blended. Spread mixture over top of tomatoes.

7. Bake at 375° for 30 minutes or until thoroughly heated. Let stand 10 minutes.

MAKES 6 servings
HANDS-ON 15 min.; **TOTAL** 1 hour, 33 min.

ZUCCHINI, SQUASH, AND CORN CASSEROLE

─────

Soft breadcrumbs double as a feather-light binder and golden crumb topping. To make them, pulse torn slices of day-old sandwich bread in the food processor.

- 1½ lb. yellow squash, cut into ¼-inch-thick slices
- 1½ lb. zucchini, cut into ¼-inch-thick slices
- ¼ cup butter, divided
- 2 cups diced sweet onion
- 2 garlic cloves, minced
- 3 cups fresh corn kernels
- 1½ cups (6 oz.) freshly shredded white Cheddar cheese
- ½ cup sour cream
- ½ cup mayonnaise
- 2 large eggs, lightly beaten
- 2 tsp. freshly ground black pepper
- 1 tsp. table salt
- 1½ cups soft, fresh breadcrumbs, divided
- 1 cup freshly grated Asiago cheese, divided

1. Preheat oven to 350°. Bring first 2 ingredients and water to cover to a boil in a Dutch oven over medium-high heat; boil 5 minutes or until crisp-tender. Drain; gently press between paper towels.

2. Melt 2 Tbsp. butter in a skillet over medium-high heat; add onion. Sauté 10 minutes or until tender. Add garlic, and sauté 2 minutes.

3. Stir together squash, onion mixture, corn, next 6 ingredients, and ½ cup each breadcrumbs and Asiago cheese just until blended. Spoon mixture into a lightly greased 13- x 9-inch baking dish.

4. Melt remaining 2 Tbsp. butter. Stir in remaining 1 cup breadcrumbs and ½ cup Asiago cheese. Sprinkle over casserole.

5. Bake at 350° for 45 to 50 minutes until golden brown and set. Let stand 15 minutes.

MAKES 8 to 10 servings
HANDS-ON 25 min.; **TOTAL** 1 hour, 30 min.

HUMMINGBIRD CAKE

─────

The most requested recipe in Southern Living *magazine history, this cake frequents covered-dish dinners all across the South, always receiving rave reviews.*

- 3 cups all-purpose flour
- 1 tsp. baking soda
- 1 tsp. table salt
- 2 cups sugar
- 1 tsp. ground cinnamon
- 3 large eggs, beaten
- 1 cup vegetable oil
- 1½ tsp. vanilla extract
- 1 (8-oz.) can crushed pineapple, undrained
- 1 cup chopped pecans
- 2 cups chopped bananas
  Cream Cheese Frosting
- ½ cup chopped pecans

1. Preheat oven to 350°. Combine first 5 ingredients in a large bowl; add eggs and oil, stirring until dry ingredients are moistened. (Do not beat.) Stir in vanilla, pineapple, 1 cup pecans, and bananas.

2. Pour batter into 3 greased and floured 9-inch round cake pans. Bake at 350° for 25 to 30 minutes or until a wooden pick inserted in center comes out clean. Cool in pans on wire racks 10 minutes; remove from pans, and cool completely on wire racks.

3. Spread Cream Cheese Frosting between layers and on top and sides of cake; sprinkle ½ cup chopped pecans on top. Store in refrigerator.

MAKES 16 servings
HANDS-ON 25 min.; **TOTAL** 1 hour, 20 min.

CREAM CHEESE FROSTING

- 1 (8-oz.) package cream cheese, softened
- ½ cup butter, softened
- 1 (16-oz.) package powdered sugar, sifted
- 1 tsp. vanilla extract

Beat cream cheese and butter at medium speed with an electric mixer until smooth. Gradually add powdered sugar, beating at low speed until light and fluffy. Stir in vanilla.

MAKES 3 cups
HANDS-ON 10 min., **TOTAL** 10 min.

SOUTHERN 'CUE

THE *SOUTHERN LIVING* PULLED PORK SANDWICH

THE ULTIMATE SMOKY, SWEET RIBS

SHOUT HALLELUJAH POTATO SALAD

CENTRAL TEXAS SLAW

SIMPLY DEVILED EGGS

THE *SOUTHERN LIVING* PULLED PORK SANDWICH

Our Test Kitchen took cues from the pros to bring pit-barbecue flavor to the backyard.

SMOKED PORK BUTT

- 1 (4- to 5-lb.) bone-in Boston butt pork roast
- ¼ cup Smoky-Sweet BBQ Rub
- 1 (8-pack) bag white-bread buns
  Chowchow (recipe at right)
  Sweet-and-Tangy Tomato Barbecue Sauce
  (recipe, facing page)

1. Trim pork roast. Rinse and pat dry. Sprinkle with Smoky-Sweet BBQ Rub; let stand at room temperature 30 minutes.

2. Prepare smoker according to manufacturer's directions, bringing internal temperature to 225° to 250°; maintain temperature 15 to 20 minutes.

3. Place pork, fattier side up, on cooking grate directly over coals in center of smoker. Cover with smoker lid. Smoke pork, maintaining temperature inside smoker between 225° and 250°, for 5 hours; turn pork, fattier side down, and smoke 2 to 3 more hours or until a meat thermometer inserted into thickest portion registers 195°.

4. Transfer to a cutting board; cool 15 minutes. Shred pork. Serve on buns with Chowchow and Sweet-and-Tangy Tomato Barbecue Sauce.

MAKES 6 to 8 servings
HANDS-ON 30 min.; **TOTAL** 8 hours, 15 min.

SMOKY-SWEET BBQ RUB

- ¼ cup kosher salt
- ¼ cup firmly packed dark brown sugar
- 2 Tbsp. plus 2 tsp. smoked paprika
- 2 Tbsp. granulated sugar
- 2 tsp. garlic powder
- 2 tsp. freshly ground black pepper
- 1 tsp. dry mustard
- 1 tsp. ground cumin
- 1 tsp. ground ginger

Stir together all ingredients. Store in an airtight container up to 1 month.

MAKES 1 cup
HANDS-ON 5 min., **TOTAL** 5 min.

CHOWCHOW

Made with cabbage, green tomatoes, and bell peppers, Chowchow is an ideal relish for a pulled pork sandwich.

- 3 cups chopped cabbage
- ¾ cup chopped onion
- ¾ cup chopped green tomatoes
- ½ cup chopped green bell pepper
- ½ cup chopped red bell pepper
- 1 Tbsp. pickling salt
- ¾ cup sugar
- ½ cup white vinegar
- ¾ tsp. mustard seeds
- ¼ tsp. celery seeds
- ¼ tsp. ground turmeric
- ½ tsp. dried crushed red pepper (optional)
- 1 jalapeño pepper, seeded and finely chopped (optional)

Stir together cabbage, onion, green tomatoes, chopped green and red bell peppers, and pickling salt. Cover; chill 2 to 8 hours. Transfer mixture to a Dutch oven. Stir in sugar, vinegar, ¼ cup water, mustard seeds, celery seeds, turmeric, and, if desired, dried crushed red pepper. Bring to a boil over medium-high heat; reduce heat to medium, and simmer 3 minutes. Cool to room temperature. Stir in jalapeño pepper, if desired. Cover and chill 1 to 8 hours before serving.

MAKES about 3 cups
HANDS-ON 25 min., **TOTAL** 4 hours

SWEET-AND-TANGY TOMATO BARBECUE SAUCE

- 1 cup ketchup
- ⅓ cup apple cider vinegar
- ¼ cup firmly packed light brown sugar
- 1 Tbsp. onion powder
- 1 Tbsp. chili powder
- 2 Tbsp. tomato paste
- 1½ Tbsp. dark molasses
- 2 tsp. freshly ground black pepper

Bring ketchup, 1 cup water, vinegar, brown sugar, onion powder, chili powder, tomato paste, dark molasses, and freshly ground pepper to a boil in a large saucepan over medium heat, stirring occasionally. Reduce heat to low; cover and cook, stirring occasionally, 25 minutes or until slightly thickened. Cool 10 minutes. Cover and chill until ready to serve. Store in refrigerator up to 1 week.

MAKES about 2 cups
HANDS-ON 10 min., **TOTAL** 45 min.

THE ULTIMATE SMOKY, SWEET RIBS

___

For tender, juicy, fall-off-the-bone good barbecue ribs, fire up your smoker—or grill.

- 2 (2½- to 3-lb.) slabs St. Louis-style pork ribs
  Smoky Dry Rub (page 308)
- 1 cup applewood smoking chips
  Rib Braising Liquid (page 308)
  Sweet-and-Spicy Barbecue Sauce (page 308)

1. Rinse ribs, and pat dry. Remove thin membrane from back of each slab by slicing into it and pulling it off. (This will make ribs more tender.) Rub both sides of ribs with Smoky Dry Rub (about 3 to 4 Tbsp. per slab), pressing gently to adhere. Wrap each slab in plastic wrap, and chill 8 to 12 hours. Soak wood chips in water 30 minutes.

2. Prepare smoker according to manufacturer's directions, bringing internal temperature to 225° to 250°; maintain temperature 15 to 20 minutes.

3. Drain wood chips, and place on coals. Remove ribs from plastic wrap, and place ribs, meat sides up, on cooking grate; cover with smoker lid.

4. Smoke ribs, maintaining temperature inside smoker between 225° and 250°, for 3½ hours.

5. Remove ribs from smoker. Place each slab, meat side down, on a large piece of heavy-duty aluminum foil. (Foil should be large enough to completely wrap slab.) Bring up edges of foil to contain liquid. Pour half of Rib Braising Liquid over each slab. Tightly wrap each slab in foil. Return slabs, meat sides down, to smoker. Cook, covered with lid, 1 to 1½ hours, checking for tenderness after 1 hour.

6. Remove ribs; unwrap and discard foil. Generously brush both sides of slabs with Sweet-and-Spicy Barbecue Sauce.

7. Return ribs to smoker, and smoke 20 minutes or until caramelized.

MAKES 4 to 6 servings
HANDS-ON 45 min.; **TOTAL** 15 hours, 10 min., including rub, braising liquid, and sauce

FOR CHARCOAL:

1. Pile hot coals on 1 side of grill, leaving other side empty. Let grill heat up, covered with grill lid, 10 minutes or until inside temperature reaches 225° to 250°. (Don't have a built-in gauge? Insert a thermometer in top air vent of grill. Stay between 225° and 250°, adjusting vent as needed.)

2. Prepare recipe as directed in Step 1. Omit Steps 2 through 4.

3. Place soaked and drained chips directly on hot coals.

4. Grill ribs, meat sides up, on unlit side of grill, covered with grill lid, 3½ hours, keeping inside grill temp between 225° and 250°. Proceed with Steps 5 and 6.

5. Return slabs to unlit side of grill, meat sides up; grill, uncovered with grill lid, 20 minutes or until caramelized.

FOR GAS:

1. Light 1 side of gas grill, heating to 250° (low) heat, leaving other side unlit. Keep inside grill temp between 225° and 250°.

2. Prepare recipe as directed in Step 1. Omit Steps 2 through 4.

3. Place soaked and drained chips in center of a 12-inch square of heavy-duty aluminum foil, and wrap tightly to form a packet. Pierce several holes in top of packet; place directly on lit side of grill.

4. Grill ribs, meat sides up, on unlit side of grill, covered with grill lid, 3½ hours, keeping inside grill temp between 225° and 250°. Proceed with Steps 5 and 6.

5. Return ribs to unlit side of grill, meat sides up; grill, covered with grill lid, 20 minutes or until caramelized.

(continued on next page)

FOR OVEN:

1. Preheat oven to 350°. Prepare recipe as directed in Step 1, omitting wood chips.

2. Remove plastic wrap from ribs. Wrap each slab, meat side down, in heavy-duty aluminum foil.

3. Bake foil-wrapped ribs, meat sides down, on a large baking sheet at 350° for 1 hour. Unwrap ribs, and pour Rib Braising Liquid over them. Rewrap in foil, and bake 1 more hour.

4. Remove ribs from oven, unwrap, and discard foil. Cool 30 minutes.

5. Position oven rack 10 inches from heat. Increase oven temperature to broil. Brush Sweet-and-Spicy Barbecue Sauce on both sides of each slab.

6. Broil ribs, meat sides up, on baking sheet about 10 inches from heat 5 to 6 minutes or until ribs are caramelized.

SMOKY DRY RUB

Cover both sides of rib slabs with Smoky Dry Rub for a bold, flavorful crust that seals in the juices of these pork ribs.

- ¼ cup firmly packed dark brown sugar
- 2 Tbsp. smoked paprika
- 1 Tbsp. kosher salt
- 2 tsp. garlic salt
- 2 tsp. chili powder
- 2 tsp. freshly ground black pepper
- 1 tsp. onion salt
- 1 tsp. celery salt
- 1 tsp. ground red pepper
- 1 tsp. ground cumin

Stir together all ingredients. Store in an airtight container at room temperature up to 1 month.

MAKES ½ cup
HANDS-ON 10 min., **TOTAL** 10 min.

RIB BRAISING LIQUID

Rib Braising Liquid, a flavorful four-ingredient mixture, is the trick for keeping ribs from drying out.

- 1 cup apple juice
- 1 Tbsp. Smoky Dry Rub (recipe at left)
- 2 tsp. balsamic vinegar
- 1 garlic clove, minced

Stir together all ingredients. Store in an airtight container in the refrigerator up to 1 week.

MAKES 1 cup
HANDS-ON 5 min., **TOTAL** 5 min.

SWEET-AND-SPICY BARBECUE SAUCE

Can't decide if you like your 'cue spicy or sweet? You get the best of both worlds with this barbecue sauce.

- ½ cup chopped sweet onion
- 2 garlic cloves, minced
- 1 jalapeño pepper, seeded and minced
- 1 Tbsp. olive oil
- 1 (32-oz.) bottle ketchup
- 1 cup firmly packed dark brown sugar
- 1 cup apple cider vinegar
- ½ cup apple juice
- ½ cup honey
- 1 Tbsp. Worcestershire sauce
- 1 tsp. kosher salt
- 1 tsp. freshly ground black pepper
- 1 tsp. celery seeds
- ½ tsp. dried crushed red pepper

Sauté first 3 ingredients in hot olive oil in a large saucepan over medium-high heat 4 to 5 minutes or until tender. Stir in ketchup and remaining ingredients. Bring to a boil, stirring occasionally. Reduce heat to low; simmer, stirring occasionally, 30 minutes. Use immediately, or refrigerate in an airtight container up to 1 month.

MAKES 5 cups
HANDS-ON 1 hour, **TOTAL** 1 hour

SHOUT HALLELUJAH POTATO SALAD

- 5 lb. Yukon gold potatoes
- 4 large hard-cooked eggs, peeled
- 1 Tbsp. table salt
- 1 cup plus 2 Tbsp. mayonnaise
- 1 cup sweet salad cube pickles, drained
- ½ cup chopped red onion
- ½ cup chopped green bell pepper
- ½ cup chopped celery
- ¼ cup chopped fresh flat-leaf parsley
- ¼ cup yellow mustard
- 1 (4-oz.) jar diced pimiento, drained
- 2 Tbsp. seasoned rice wine vinegar
- 2 Tbsp. fresh lemon juice
- 1 Tbsp. extra virgin olive oil
- 1 to 2 jalapeño peppers, seeded and minced
- 1 to 2 tsp. celery salt
- 4 drops of hot sauce
- ½ tsp. smoked paprika
  Freshly ground black pepper

1. Cook potatoes in boiling water to cover about 20 minutes or until tender; drain and cool 15 minutes. Peel potatoes, and place in a large bowl. Add eggs, and chop mixture into bite-size pieces. Sprinkle with salt; toss to coat.

2. Stir mayonnaise and next 13 ingredients together; gently stir into potato mixture. Sprinkle with paprika; add black pepper to taste. Serve immediately, or cover and chill up to 2 days.

MAKES 12 servings
HANDS-ON 25 min., **TOTAL** 1 hour

CENTRAL TEXAS SLAW

This slaw gets its kick and Southwestern flair from the jalapeño pepper and cilantro.

- ¼ cup white vinegar
- ¼ cup extra virgin olive oil
- 2 Tbsp. sugar
- 3 to 4 Tbsp. fresh lime juice
- 1½ tsp. kosher salt
- ½ tsp. ground coriander
- ¼ tsp. ground cumin
- ¼ tsp. ground red pepper
- ¼ tsp. freshly ground black pepper
- 2 cups thinly sliced red cabbage
- 2 cups thinly sliced bok choy (Chinese white cabbage)
- ½ cup shredded carrot
- 1 medium jalapeño pepper (with seeds), thinly sliced
- ½ red bell pepper, thinly sliced
- ½ yellow bell pepper, thinly sliced
- ½ cup chopped fresh cilantro

Whisk together first 9 ingredients in a large bowl. Add red cabbage, bok choy, carrot, jalapeño pepper, red bell pepper, and yellow bell pepper. Toss to coat. Chill 1 hour before serving, tossing occasionally. Stir in cilantro before serving.

MAKES about 4 cups
HANDS-ON 15 min.; **TOTAL** 1 hour, 15 min.

SIMPLY DEVILED EGGS

- 12 large eggs
- ⅓ cup fat-free Greek yogurt
- 2 oz. ⅓-less-fat cream cheese
- 1 Tbsp. chopped fresh parsley
- 1 tsp. Dijon mustard
- ⅛ tsp. table salt

1. Place eggs in a single layer in a stainless steel saucepan. (Do not use nonstick.) Add water to depth of 3 inches. Bring to a rolling boil; cook 1 minute. Cover, remove from heat, and let stand 10 minutes. Drain.

2. Place eggs under cold running water until just cool enough to handle. Tap eggs on the counter until cracks form; peel.

3. Slice eggs in half lengthwise; carefully remove yolks. Mash together yolks, yogurt, and next 4 ingredients until smooth using a fork. Spoon yolk mixture into egg white halves. Serve immediately, or cover and chill 1 hour before serving.

MAKES 2 dozen
HANDS-ON 25 min., **TOTAL** 40 min.

5 NEW DEVILED EGG FAVORITES

Try these innovative stir-ins to make your own signature deviled eggs. Prepare recipe at left as directed, stirring one of the following delicious combos into yolk mixture (Step 3).

1. Creole Shrimp: ½ cup finely chopped cooked shrimp, 3 Tbsp. sautéed chopped green bell pepper, 1 minced green onion, ¼ tsp. Creole seasoning, ¼ tsp. hot sauce. Top with cooked shrimp.

2. Texas Caviar: 3 Tbsp. chopped roasted red bell pepper, 1 minced green onion, 1 Tbsp. minced pickled jalapeño pepper, 1 Tbsp. chopped fresh cilantro, 1 tsp. Italian dressing mix. Top with canned black-eyed peas and fresh cilantro leaves.

3. High Society: ½ cup cooked fresh lump crabmeat, 2 tsp. fresh tarragon, ½ tsp. lemon zest, ¼ tsp. freshly ground black pepper. Top with cooked fresh crabmeat and watercress.

4. Georgia Peach: 3 Tbsp. peach preserves, ¼ cup finely chopped country ham, 1 tsp. grated Vidalia onion, ½ tsp. apple cider vinegar, ¼ tsp. freshly ground black pepper. Top with sliced fresh peaches and chopped toasted pecans.

5. Triple Pickle: 3 Tbsp. chopped bread-and-butter pickles, 2 Tbsp. chopped capers. Top with pickled okra slices.

SUBJECT INDEX

RECIPE INDEX

ESSAYISTS' BIOGRAPHIES

STEVEN BENDER is a Senior Editor at *Southern Living* and writes "The Grumpy Gardener" column for the magazine.

JOHN CURRENCE opened his award-winning restaurant, City Grocery, in Oxford, Mississippi, in 1992. He is the author of *Pickles, Pigs & Whiskey* and a contributing editor to *Garden & Gun*.

JOHN HUEY, an Atlantan born and raised, is a former editor in chief of Time Inc.

BOBBY McALPINE is an architect and principle in the distinguished firms McAlpine Booth & Ferrier Interiors and McAlpine Tankersley Architecture.

JULIA REED was born in the Mississippi Delta. She is the author of several books, including *Queen of the Turtle Derby and Other Southern Phenomena* and *But Mama Always Put Vodka in Her Sangria!: Adventures in Eating, Drinking, and Making Merry.*

APRIL REYNOLDS teaches creative writing at Sarah Lawrence College and is the author of the award-winning novel *Knee-Deep in Wonder.*

JANE AND MICHAEL STERN are contributing editors at *Saveur* magazine and weekly guests on Public Radio's award-winning "The Splendid Table." Their website, Roadfood.com, reviews 2000 of America's greatest regional restaurants.

ACKNOWLEDGMENTS

THE EDITORS GRATEFULLY ACKNOWLEDGE the support of Sid Evans and the current *Southern Living* staff, as well as the many "alumni" who so generously volunteered their time, photographs, and memorabilia to help us capture the essence of the magazine.

SPECIAL THANKS to John Floyd, Clay Nordan, Jean Wickstrom Liles, Philip Morris, John Logue, Mary Allen Perry, Dianne Young, Martha Johnston, and Mark Sandlin for their guidance, regional insights, and historical context; special thanks also to Peggy Smith, Karen Lingo, Caleb Pirtle, Susan Dosier, Susan Payne Dobbs, Judy Feagin, Deborah Garrison Lowery, Bill McDougald, Lil Petrusnek, Gene Bussell, and Gary Wright for valuable advice and enough great stories to fill several books.

WE ARE DEEPLY INDEBTED to the Eugene Butler Papers, as well as other historical holdings of the Southern Progress Corporation Archives, including *Life at Southern Living: A Sort of Memoir*, by John Logue and Gary McCalla (Louisiana State University Press, 2000). Many thanks to Nellah McGough and Jason Burnett for helping us navigate this archival material and to April Smitherman for outstanding research assistance.

©2015 Time Inc. Books
1271 Avenue of the Americas, New York, NY 10020

ISBN-13: 978-0-8487-4414-4
ISBN-10: 0-8487-4414-4
Library of Congress Control Number: 2015942383

Printed in China
First Printing 2015

Creative Director: Felicity Keane
Senior Editor: Katherine Cobbs
Editor: Susan Hernandez Ray
Art Director: Christopher Rhoads
Executive Photography Director: Iain Bagwell
Photography Editor: Kellie Lindsey
Assistant Managing Editor: Jeanne de Lathouder
Assistant Designer: Allison Sperando Potter
Editorial Assistant: April Smitherman
Senior Production Manager: Greg A. Amason
Production Manager: Terri Beste Farley
Assistant Production Manager: Diane Rose Keener
Assistant Production Director: Sue Chodakiewicz

CONTRIBUTORS
Writer: Valerie Fraser Luesse
Editor: Leslie Stoker
Junior Designer: AnnaMaria Jacob
Assistant Project Editor: Megan Thompson Brown
Photographer: Stephen DeVries
Food Stylists: Marian Cooper Cairns, Ana Kelly
Photo Stylist: Lydia DeGaris Pursell
Photo Researcher: Julie Claire
Copy Editor: Donna Baldone
Proofreader: Rebecca Brennan
Indexer: Mary Ann Laurens
Editorial Fellows: Kylie Dazzo, Nicole Fisher

SOUTHERN LIVING
Editor in Chief: Sid Evans
Creative Director: Robert Perino
General Manager: Whitney Wright
Senior Executive Editor: Katy McColl
Art Director: Paul Carstensen
Executive Editor: Jessica S. Thuston
Deputy Editor: Jennifer V. Cole
Copy Chief: Susan Emack Alison
Director of Photography: Jeanne Dozier Clayton
Photographers: Robbie Caponetto, Laurey W. Glenn,
   Alison Miksch, Hector Sanchez
Office Manager: Nellah Bailey McGough

PHOTO CREDITS